ELEMENTS *OF* *GOOD & HAPPY* MARRIAGES

MVELO TABENI

Elements of Good & Happy Marriages

Published by Mvelo Tabeni

P.O. Box 21387, Gqeberha, 6000, Nelson Mandela Bay, South Africa.

Mvelo.Tabeni@gmail.com

First edition 2022

ISBN 978-0-6397-2947-3

Cover design and typesetting by Wade Hunkin (wade@printondemand.co.za)

Set in Garamond 14/17

CONTENTS

IS YOUR MARRIAGE GOOD AND HAPPY?

IF NOT, IT'S TIME TO EMBRACE CHANGE.

ACKNOWLEDGEMENTS

I am extremely grateful to Pastor Marius Gradwell, Pastor Khaya Maphinda and Mr Mbulelo Maxwell Ngewu (Marriage Counsellor), for not giving up on this project and on me. Many thanks for their unwavering support into this project and for their hard work to make it a reality. I am also grateful to Mr Lwando Bantom for all of his support and encouragement. Special thanks to my wife Thuli and my three sons Monwabisi, Apiwe and Vuyo for believing in my project and supporting me during my season of writing. The dream of this book would not have been possible without this special family surrounding me with their love and support.

FOREWORD

Marriage is God's idea, therefore He blessed it. He said, *"Be fruitful, multiply and fill the earth".* Marriage is a gift from God. Husband and wife are a gift to one another to enjoy. A good and happy marriage is a gift to their children, and they are beneficiaries because their parents follow God's plan. A good marriage brings heaven to earth, God's gift to the world. Marriages were made in heaven, but they must be worked out here on earth. Marriage has enemies, one is the devil who hates what God loves and always opposes God's plan and design. The other is the unredeemed nature of man. Selfishness amongst couples has destroyed many marriages, and it remains a major challenge for present day marriages.

"Elements of Good and Happy Marriages" is an excellent and practical tool to help with the "working out" of marriage. It is like a mirror to look into, it will help to reveal the true condition of your marriage, but at the same time it will encourage you and guide you to a Good and Happy Marriage.

The quizzes after each chapter are very helpful and they encourage transparency and honesty. I would encourage married couples to read and work through this book together.

Furthermore, I would suggest that mature married couples make use of *"Elements of Good and Happy Marriages"*, as they disciple younger married couples and soon to be married couples as well.

I am delighted that Mvelo has heeded the unction of God to help, save and strengthen marriages by writing this book. I thank God for his courage!

MARIUS GRADWELL, Pastor

PREFACE

God has a plan for our marriages. It is our duty to seek it, find it, embrace it and live it. The intention of this book is to encourage married couples to internalize the elements of good and happy marriages in their own marital relationships. Such internalization will advance or step-up the couples' abilities to confront everyday marriage challenges with confidence. This could be done through the power of a meaningful dialogue and commitment to improve on the elements of good and happy marriages. The world-wide statistics on marriage sustenance is not good and favorable, hence I felt the need to play this important part of encouraging the married couples to be the best that they can be in their relationships. I have made a strong mitigation for marriage sustenance in the discussion of the *"Elements of Good and Happy Marriages"*, in the interest of married couples.

The secret of spouses is in finding solutions through significant conversation, having understood the context of marriage; and the fact that the human being is the most sophisticated and complicated element of that context. I am of the opinion that it would be very difficult to take best and appropriate decisions for situations which we do not know and understand. The better understanding of the context of marriage, will assist the couples to know exactly what they are dealing with in their relationships. I articulate in part the context of marriage by discussing the elements of good and happy marriages. The undeniable reality is that these elements unpack the intricate marriage context especially to the married people.

This context is full of toxins that bring toxicity into the relationship, that is one of the reasons why married couples have to constantly work on their marriages in order to deal with the toxins. ***In actual fact, to put it correctly I should say that, the couples should constantly work on themselves in order to deal with the toxicity that troubles their marriages.*** It is the married couples who should understand, internalize and put into practice the elements of good and happy marriages in their own relationships.

The reality is that the challenges are not in the air, they emanate from the marriage partners themselves. The elements in discussion form part of what the married couples need to positively address, with the aim of keeping peace and tranquility prevalent in the relationship. Frequent improvement on these elements will also ensure the sustainability of happiness and peace in the relationship. I hope that would also be the benefit of your own marriage relationship as well.

The elements of good and happy marriages are the bedrock of the entire discussion in this book. These elements allude to the context of marriage throughout all the ensuing chapters. Elements refer to fundamentals, features, ingredients, parts or components of a bigger thing; and the bigger thing in the context of this book is the marriage. In actual fact, these elements are bits and pieces or the odds and ends that make up our marriages.

In the detailed discussion within *"Elements of Good & Happy Marriages"* I talk about how to work towards having resilient, healthy and happy marriages in such a time as this. The write-up also emphasizes problem confrontation through the power of dialogue. ***Hence I mention a researched fact which states that, couples who are living healthy and happy marriages are the ones who are the masters of dialogue.*** Happiness and sustenance of your marriage is in your hands and not even in a marriage counselors' hands, but in your own hands as a married couple. You have to ask God to give you wisdom and help your hands to handle your marriage relationship with care. The elements are being discussed in such a way that they will also be assisting you to handle your relationship with maximum care.

Another purpose of writing *"Elements of Good & Happy Marriages"* is to encourage resilience in marriage relationships; where the word *"resilient"* means the ability to recover quickly from difficult conditions. When our marriage relationships happen to fall apart, God is not to blame but we are. It is my hope that the book will encourage you and positively influence the way you think about your marriage relationship. This should also boost the contribution of dialogue to you as a couple in a very meaningful way. In other words, I aim to minimize the *"withdrawal syndrome"* of avoiding one another as married partners during time of difficulty, and at the same time maximize reasoning together when time and situations demand that amongst couples. ***The focus should be on finding quality solutions to marital challenges through conversation among the couples themselves.***

The quizzes after each chapter are meant to encourage the readers to reflect, and also trigger a useful dialogue amongst the couples; because the quizzes have a potential to reveal the strong points and also indicate areas of weakness in the relationships for the couples' attention. The dialogue should make the couples to come up with their own solutions to the problem areas of their marriages, as identified in each of the elements in discussion. It is limitless what the couples can do to make their marriage relationships good and happy.

There's a myriad of positive things that they can do for their marriages during their life time. That's one reason why couples get tired along the way. However, it is better to be doing something no matter how small, than being found doing nothing about our marriage relationships. Sometimes doing nothing is even worse than failing.

The entire discussion is all about working towards good and happy marriage relationships. ***Marriages are meant to be long term love relationships that have to be enjoyed as long as the couples live.*** They are never meant to be a life of frustration and misery, but the reality is that the marriage relationships are also never problem free. Otherwise life would not be fun and exciting. Working on the marriage relationship is a life time exercise, so please, do not rush through it or else you will get tired. Just move along with it as you live your life as a couple. Enjoy the reading.

INTRODUCTION

Research shows that happy and long lasting marriages are the ones who are also doing well in most of the elements discussed in the chapters that follow. Long term happiness doesn't just happen over you in the marriage relationship, you need to work on it just like a beautiful and lovable flower garden. If no one cares the flowers die.

Somebody once said to me, *"It seems there's a lot to do to keep our marriages alive, and we will never get to do all of it, and so, we will all fail as married couples."* ***I suppose that, it is not about rushing to do it all, but doing what you have to do when it is necessary to do it.*** In a nutshell, it's about taking one step at a time. Happiness in our marriage relationships is not only about getting all that we want, but it is also derived from enjoying all that we already have.

When there is unhappiness in the marriage, it is not really the marriage that has to change; but the people of the marriage in the marriage. Let me reiterate and also expatiate on that, marriage on its own is pure, holy and innocent so to speak. However, the context within which the marriage lives has to change for the better, and the human beings are the greater part of that context. My critical thinking has most often pushed my mind to the point of curiosity to know *"Why"*. Why are some marriages happy and others not? Why is the world-wide divorce rate so high? I always wanted to know the *"Why"* part of things that are not going okay, especially concerning marriage relationships. These are some of the critical things I will talk about in the chapters that follow.

The married couple's relationship is a collaborative effort and one partner will not succeed alone, as it takes two to "tango". You need to ensure that you always collaborate with your partner to work on your relationship. Sometimes, even when the couple seems to be competing with each other for resources or ambitious achievements, they are unavoidably and undeniably part of a collective effort and they can't run away from it. This collective effort aims to grow, maintain and sustain the overall well-being of their marriage and family. ***No one else can do it better than them, and if they fail, their marriage and the family will suffer.***

Having a lack of the elements of good and happy marriages will influence the nature of the marriage relationship towards the bad side of things; whilst having the abundance of them will influence the relationship to the good and positive side. The married couples have to constantly work on these good elements for their marriage relationship to positively and successfully grow. This will also help the couple from growing apart and becoming bored and hostile strangers, who cannot tolerate to live together anymore. ***Happy families have these good elements in practice and as a way of life in their marriage relationships.*** When the partners are actively working on the mentioned elements, they are likely to feel most useful to each other in the relationship.

On the other hand, an unhappy marriage relationship doesn't mean your marriage is doomed, and that it ended a long time ago and you were just not aware of it. That is one lie that couples should not believe. The reality is that ***marriage relationships get less happy over a period of time,*** and that is one reason why the partners must constantly work on their relationships. This book is just about that, and working on these elements of good and happy marriages is really about ***"making what matters matter."***

The work on these elements might seem a lot of work but my take is that, work on one element at a time. That is necessary for the marriage relationship to remain healthy, happy and strong. Remember that ***married life is much more complicated than the life of singleness,*** because the relationship is between two different individuals deciding to live a shared life together for the rest of their life time; and that demands the couple to work on their marriage relationship for it to remain healthy and happy. That is just like the body work-outs which the body needs in order to be healthy and strong. These elements also gather and join the two of you towards a common purpose, and improve your commitment in all levels of your marriage life.

This discussion on the elements of good and happy marriages has been inspired by my courage to advocate moral characters among the married couples. Deciding to rate yourself on each element and committing to improve on each one will not only make a difference in your life, but also in the life of your partner. Your marriage life will be transformed for the better when that happens. Have fun with the reading and enjoy doing the quizzes and talking about them with your partner. The fact of the matter is that ***the much needed change in the marriage relationship starts with each spouse.***

One other thing that has motivated me to my write-up is the flawless public façade of modern day marriages which has masked its private despair. The statistics on marriages tells it all to assure us of this fact, and it cannot be hidden to the one who wants to see it. I am of the view that putting into practice the elements of good and happy marriages, will also improve the quality of life among the couples. Some of us suffer from depression, stress, anxiety and so forth as result of depressed marriage relationships. ***It is worth it to embrace and pursue the things that contribute to your well-being.*** That is a noble purpose in a couple's life time, no one can afford to miss that invaluable opportunity.

The following is a list of the elements of good and happy marriages which have been considered for discussion. I expanded on them based on my three-pronged approach of Biblical background, Life experiences and Findings from the world of Behavioral studies.

ELEMENTS OF GOOD & HAPPY MARRIAGES	
1.	Love
2.	Trust
3.	Commitment
4.	Making Time, Attention & Having Fun
5.	Good Communication & Listening
6.	Partnership & Doing Things Together
7.	Tolerance, Honesty & Patience
8.	Respect
9.	Consideration & Openness
10.	Sharing & Generosity
11.	Money Matters
12.	Willingness to Compromise
13.	Embracing Constructive Criticism
14.	Good Management of Arguments
15.	Willingness to Hear your Partner's View Point
16.	Ability and Willingness to Forgive
17.	Willingness to Apologize
18.	Showing Empathy, Sympathy & Responsiveness
19.	Praying Together

CHAPTER 1

LOVE

God is love and there is no greater love than the love God portrayed to humankind. Even the burning love of couples in a marriage relationship, cannot be compared to the perfect and unconditional love that God has for humankind. That sets a good example as to how we should aim to love one another as couples. The true love includes the admiration, care and respect of your marriage partner; and never subjecting your partner to humiliation, harm, hurt or any form of abuse. The Bible's definition of love comes in different ways; love can be made a living organism by personifying it or it can be described as a personal value. Just listen to the following quotes equitably:

"[4]Love is patient and kind. Love is not jealous or boastful or proud [5]or rude. It does not demand its own way. It is not irritable, and it keeps no record of being wronged. [6]It does not rejoice about injustice but rejoices whenever the truth wins out. [7]Love never gives up, never loses faith, is always hopeful, and endures through every circumstance. [8]Prophecy and speaking in unknown languages and special knowledge will become useless. But love will last forever!" (1 Corinthians 13:4-8 NLT).

"A new commandment I give to you, that you love one another; as I have loved you, that you also love one another." (John 13:34 NKJV).

One has to understand that genuine love is sacrificial to the benefit of the other spouse.

"But God demonstrates His own love toward us, in that while we were still sinners, Christ died for us."
(Romans 5:8 NKJV).

In a fair-minded manner, think about this deeply; when we were in our own sins and crooked ways, and not even thinking about serving God, yet He loved you and me right at that point in time. That kind of love constrains me to love Him back in earnest.

The relationship lesson here is that whilst the one spouse is in error, making mistakes and caring less, the other spouse continues to love and support. ***Love your partner with passion and compassion, don't fake it even for one time. Spouses who are gradually and constantly doing something to make and keep each other happy, they are the ones who keep the freshness in the marriage relationship.*** That's a healthy practice for the relationship's benefit. We should all learn to maintain that reciprocity with diligence. According to Oxford languages dictionary, Love is defined as an intense feeling for deep affection. This portrays that there is an emotional attachment or connection. Let me then deduce from that and say, ***"As a couple, the happier you are with the relationship, the deeper the affection and vice versa."*** I also concur with the fact that everyone gives and receives love differently.

"And so we know and rely on the love God has for us. God is love. Whoever lives in love lives in God, and God in them."
(1 Jn. 4:16).

"Do everything in love."
(1 Cor. 16:14).

Consummate or Complete Love

When I was reading and investigating about love, I came across eight different types of human love. However, I decided to choose only 3 which I found to be very much relevant to my discussion of the context of marriage, in terms of the elements of good and happy marriages. In actual fact, one of the three is the ***"Rolls Royce"*** of love that every couple aims for but not many will ever get there, because it is rare to find in our day and age. Some psychologists call it the ***"gold standard of relationships."*** This type is called Pragma in ancient Greek, which is closely defined as enduring love. It is also called ***Consummate love*** which is the complete form of human love. According to Robert Sternberg's theory, this kind of love requires a perfect balance among high levels of intimacy, passion and commitment.

Even in the context of marriage, this represents the ideal relationship towards which many couples aim, but apparently few may attain it. Actually, Sternberg gives prudence that maintaining such love may be even harder than achieving it. It is also said by other researchers that couples with this type of love share a deep desire to be together on every level, even after many years. ***It is said to be the strongest and most enduring type of love relationship.***

My take on this is that, I see this kind of love being the closest to what is mentioned in 1 Cor. 13 of the Holy Writ. This is not it but very close to it, because this passage talks about God who is love and that kind of love is our model to look towards when we are practically trying to love each other, even as married couples. Then, this leaves me to talk about the other two types of love which are the very much prevalent among couples.

Using the knowledge based approach I wish to mention other two types of love as generally known to be Romantic Love (passionate) and Affectionate Love (compassionate), which are very much prevalent in relationships today.

Romantic Love

It is also referred to as ***passionate love***. This type of love is said to have strong components of intimacy and passion but lacks commitment. The partners spend much time with each other enjoying their closeness and companionship; but have not made plans for a permanent stay of their affair, this part is specific to the unmarried. Sexuality and physicality are often dominant in this part of a love relationship, as passionate love involves intense feelings and sexual attraction.

However, this is nowhere near to the type of love mentioned in 1 Cor. 13. In terms of benefits, some researchers state that being loved upholds our sense of self-esteem, conquers shame-based doubts about our state and condition of being lovable, and alleviates or soothes our fears of loneliness. They also admit that romantic love is not the most important love of all. However, they also allude to the fact that Romantic love can last a lifetime and contribute to happier, healthier relationships among couples. To me, this puts emphasis on the fact that couples should not do away or neglect the romantic aspect in their marriage relationships, it still plays a big lifetime role.

On the other hand, they should also understand that ***romance alone cannot sustain the health and happiness of the marriage relationship.*** This tells me that even romantic love cools down after a period of time. The behavioral researchers state that the honeymoon stage can last up to two years, at which point, the overwhelming feelings of love and happiness begin to fade or cool down.

I have been wondering for some time as to which organ of the human body is love turned on, until I bumped against some of the researched love theories. I chose to concur with the researchers that suggest that love is turned on from the mind or brain. Often times the craziness of romantic love takes over from logic, you can imagine what happens thereafter. Hence the emphasis to take things slowly at one step at a time during the early stages of the love relationship, specifically in the pre-marital relationships.

Once the partners lose logic to passion in the relationship, things are bound not to go in the right direction. So, be warned and let logic prevail in order to get passion under control. Bear in mind, the mind is doing all the hard spinning whilst the heart is just beating the drums. Psychological studies mention that the brain is very much in control of romance and not the heart. It is further stated that love relates to our brains more than our hearts. However, what happens in the mind concerning love affects the heart, perhaps causing it to beat the drums faster. You should also be mindful of the fact that our emotional responses are controlled from the mind.

Compassionate Love

This is also referred to as *affectionate love*. It is the type of love that occurs when individuals desire to have the other person near and have a deep caring effect for the person. (desire of living together as one). Sexuality and infatuation are not the prevailing elements of this kind of love, but companionship is very much prevalent. One spouse's presence in the life of the other makes the other to feel complete in the presence of the other. Compassionate love involves feelings of mutual respect, trust, and affection towards the other person.

This is the type of love that also comes close to the love mentioned in 1 Cor. 13. There's a number of theories coming from the world of research about love. The behavioral researchers state that the theory of ***compassionate love*** is characterized by trust and companionship, while passionate love is more physical and sexual. They also allude to the finding that ***passionate love*** typically simmers down to compassionate love within one to two years, under normal circumstances.

I have learnt that compassionate love is not limited to spouses or love partners. The Greeks also define this kind of love as *"affectionate love."* In other words, it is the kind of love that you also feel for your friends. It is a deep liking and adoration towards a few people we have in our lives. It is the love that makes us go to great lengths for the people we love. Compassionate love is also termed *"platonic love"* named after the Greek philosopher Plato. Platonic love is said to involve deep affection, but no romantic or sexual attraction. This also means love without sexual acts, hence it is also referred to as the love that you have for your friends. Now I understand why people in the secular world would say, *"Let us not be lovers for now, but let us be friends, just friends."*

Let's look at the researchers' key difference between love and compassion which states that, love is a deep feeling of affection and attachment towards someone, whereas compassion is a sympathetic pity and concern for the sufferings or misfortunes of others. Compassion literally means *"to suffer together."* So, when you add the two words together this is what you get;

Love + Compassion = Compassionate Love

In terms of tenacity, this one becomes the pertinacious of relationships, I mean the mighty conqueror of challenges and the real sustainer of marriage relationships.

What does the Bible say about love and compassion?

"Love is patient and kind; love does not envy or boast; it is not arrogant or rude."
(1 Cor. 13).

"And now abideth faith, hope, love, these three; but the greatest of these is love."
(1 Cor. 13:13).

"Be kind and compassionate to one another, forgiving each other, just as in Christ God forgave you."
(Eph. 4:32).

When comparing men and women, researchers found that men fall in love more easily than women. They also discovered that men do not end relationships quicker and more easily as women do. Besides, both of them share the same common ground; ***"They aim and desire for the compassionate love".*** Their difference is the angle from which they stand looking to what they are aiming at. (the desired situation). That is why they use different approaches to get there.

In the process some people may mistakenly think romantic love to be compassionate love, or see no difference between the two. Whereas, the reality is that everyone gives and receives love differently. This is what a couple needs to understand about each other.

Some psychologists put it this way, *"Women are wired differently compared to men".* Their destination is the same but they use different ways to get there. ***One spouse***

has to show to the other that he or she is needed in the relationship. When one spouse tells the other that, *"I can do better without you."* That is one sign that compassionate love is lacking and selfishness is prevalent.

Selfishness is what causes the two partners not to understand each other. Compassionate love is the love that says, "You are the bone of my bones, the flesh of my flesh, and I am incomplete without you in this relationship of ours, together we suffer and together we win."

Genuine love compels a partner to take action for the other partner. Just listen to the following passage where Peter had to do something to show his love for his master;

"15 After breakfast Jesus asked Simon Peter, "Simon son of John, do you love me more than these?"

"Yes, Lord," Peter replied, "you know I love you."

"Then feed my lambs," Jesus told him.

16 Jesus repeated the question: "Simon son of John, do you love me?"

"Yes, Lord," Peter said, "you know I love you."

"Then take care of my sheep," Jesus said.

17 A third time he asked him, "Simon son of John, do you love me?"

Peter was hurt that Jesus asked the question a third time. He said, "Lord, you know everything. You know that I love you." Jesus said, "Then feed my sheep."

18 "I tell you the truth, when you were young, you were able to do as you liked; you dressed yourself and went wherever

you wanted to go. But when you are old, you will stretch out your hands, and others will dress you and take you where you don't want to go."
(John 21:15-18 NLT).

That compassionate love for your partner teaches you to be a perseverant. I mean real indefatigability when it comes to giving up on your partner; even the temperament spams from either partner will never conquer the compassionate love that you have for each other. She may even rich the boiling point or she may become speechless with rage, that means nothing to the power of compassionate love. He may roar like an angry and hungry lion but compassionate love is bigger and louder than that.

The famous verse of John 3:16 tells us that God so loved the world such that He gave His only begotten son, for our salvation from the brutal life of sin. He didn't give up on the sinful you and me while He had all the good reasons to do it. ***His love for us was never conquered by our bad life of sin and stubbornness.***

The couple needs to learn a thing or two from God's love as to how to love each other, regardless of the stubbornness towards the wrong direction by one partner. The crucial fact is that when you know that you got married with someone that you compassionately love, you will easily be able to overlook and accommodate the mistakes or even his or her imperfections so to speak. ***The compassionate love is the love that keeps on loving even when one partner is doing the unlovable things.*** However, the compassionate love is also corrective towards the wrong partner, also in a compassionate manner for your amazement.

Let me close this chapter by talking about the ***"stubborn"*** love. Remember that God loved us when we were still sinners. (Rom. 5:8). The condition that we were in never changed His perfect love towards us. The love that God has for us is so powerful such that it made Him to do something for our sinful condition instead of rejecting and destroying us, when we were unlovable so to speak. ***Our sinful condition never made God to have a second thought about His love for sinful mankind.***

If we take Christ Jesus as the biggest role model of our lives, then we should follow suite. If one married somebody because she is a talented singer or he is a gifted musical instrument player or a gifted preacher; someday one may find her in deep sleep snoring badly. When one doesn't like what he sees he may feel like saying, ***"Sweetheart, it would be better for you to wake up and sing."*** And the reason being, singing is what he loves in her and not her bad snoring. Then the second case would be the lady who would say to her snoring spouse, ***"Honey, it would be better for you to wake up and play the piano or preach a sermon for me."*** And the reason being, those are the things she loves in him and not his bad snoring. When you love a person you love him or her with all the imperfections, bad snoring included.

The unpleasant or the not so good habits of your loved one should not change your love that you have towards him or her. If the opposite happens it may mean that your love is not compassionate enough in terms of maturity, you still need to work on it. When you love each other compassionately, it means that you love each other regardless of the unpleasant habits of one another.

I mean regardless of the deep sleep bad snoring. As one would find his cute little baby snoring, one should also just smile by finding his partner in deep sleep and snoring. Compassionately loving each other also means that you are saying, *"We discovered that we are mutually compatible and we can harmoniously live with each other."*

ANALOGY QUIZ: LOVE			
No.	**ASSESSMENT STATEMENTS** (where 10 is most likely and 5 means it needs some tender loving attention)	**10**	**5**
1.	In our marriage relationship, compassionate love matters the most.		
2.	Our (romantic) passionate love is not stronger than our (affectionate) compassionate love.		
3.	Our (affectionate) compassionate love is stronger that our (romantic) passionate love.		
4.	I am romantic in our relationship.		
5.	My partner is romantic in our relationship.		
6.	I am very compassionate in our relationship.		
7.	My partner is very compassionate in our relationship.		
8.	Which type of love shows more weaknesses and needs some nurturing in our relationship? Romantic or Compassionate. (please tick the appropriate one)	Rom	Com
9.	Which type of love do I want to dominate our marriage relationship? Romantic or Compassionate. (please tick the appropriate one)	Rom	Com
10.	My partner loves me regardless of my shortcomings, and I know it.		

11.	I love my partner regardless of his or her shortcomings, and he/she knows it.		
12.	I support my partner and he/she supports me, and we both make each other to feel important in the relationship.		

Quiz Notes:
The quiz has 10 items for scoring and having an overall score of 100 means you are doing just fine in this *"element"* as far as the 10 items are concerned; and there is minimal enhancement or improvement to be done. In statement 8 & 9 you don't have to score but you choose the applicable type of love to reflect your preferences and then discuss it as partners about what you've chosen. A score below 100-80 (80%) means tender loving attention is required on all items that scored a 5. A score of 50 (50%) and below means that definitely one has to do a lot of work to reach the confidence level on this *"element"*. One has to do some serious introspection, and then further engage in a meaningful dialogue with the spouse. If things seem to be overwhelming, you still have the professional counselor on your side for guidance. Remember, the quiz is not the counselor, it only gives clues to say among others; what things you need to consider on your way to making your marriage happy as far as the element of Love is concerned.

CHAPTER 2

TRUST

In terms of definition from Oxford languages dictionary taking it in the context of marriage, trust is defined as the ***firm belief in the ability or reliability of your partner to deliver*** on his or her agreed upon responsibilities in the marriage relationship. In the case of an example, a partner should trust the ability and reliability of another partner that he or she will be loyal to the vows of the marriage relationship. ***Trust is not manufactured overnight, but it is built over a period of time between the partners through experience.*** At times it may be breached and then take a lot time to rebuild it successfully. ***The more it is breached and broken, the less likely are the chances to rebuild it to be stronger than before successfully.*** This tells me that trust is a frangible matter but also a powerful tool in the sustenance of the marriage relationship. Frangible implies susceptibility to being broken into fragments without implying weakness or delicacy. So, trust is strong and not weak but frangible.

The issue of trust is very deep such that I would like to do a bit of analogy whilst trying to expatiate on it, using the similitude of trust to a cup which is later broken into four mendable pieces. Let's take the example of the ceramic cup that might have fallen several times without breaking, but there comes a time when the same cup will fall and break. Let's say it breaks into four pieces which are mendable. The four pieces are not what you want, but you want a complete cup that you can use for its real purpose. Remember, a complete cup has a purpose but the four broken pieces have no purpose, because you can't drink from them but you can from a complete cup. So, a broken trust does not serve any good purpose in the marriage relationship, unless the pieces of the broken trust are put together again.

The breakability of the cup depends on how high is the height from where it falls, and how hard is the surface on which it falls. Another important factor would be if it's a mended cup from previous down falls, that would make it more vulnerable than before. Now you can imagine, the situation becomes scary as it moves from just frangible to be fragile, which indicates weakness and to be easily breakable. There is now more likelihood that the "four mended pieces cup" may break into more than four pieces this time due to higher height and harder surface of the fall. This may become a reality of life in one's marriage relationship. The crux of the matter is that trust should not be ***"taken too lightly"*** by the married couples such that it becomes a thing of being broken more often than not.

The situational irony, paradox or incongruity in marriage relationships is that; there will also be hope to mend the broken pieces of the ceramic cup no matter how many pieces it's broken into. The situation may also be such that even if the cup has been grinded into ceramic powder, there's always hope to build a new cup from the powder itself again.

However, the fact of the matter is that, the frequency of breakages nullifies the chances of possible mending of the ceramic cup, but understandably, humans are humans and not ceramic; and there is also an element of faith in God which is only attached to human beings. We are talking about dynamic creatures made after God's own image. ***Again, let me say that, trust in itself is very strong and never weak***

nor fragile, but frangible and only when made vulnerable. The reason I say this is that, even when it is said to have been broken between two spouses, it has enough power to be resuscitated when all hopes are gone to get it alive again. It's all about choices of giving each other 2nd, 3rd, 4th, or even 5th chance as we feel like as marriage partners. It is also about saying what you mean and meaning what you say.

Trust is also defined as a firm belief in the character, strength and truth of your partner. The basics of trust are simple but very challenging to effectuate. Some of these are:

- Being loyal and dependable to your spouse
- Keeping your word, no matter how small
- Being honest and transparent in your expressions to your partner
- Being there when your partner needs you

The matter of truthfulness to one another as a couple starts even before the marriage union. The understanding is that no one should get into marriage with a lie because one will live a life of lies. In each and every time that the hidden truth is about to come out one will have to cover it with a lie. Eventually the hidden truth will come out at some point in time, even after 10 or 20 years in marriage. It is better for each partner to be open and tell the other everything that has to be known even way before the wedding preparations, let alone the wedding day or thereafter; not even to mention during marriage life, the couple cannot afford to live a life of lies. The weakness of trust between the partners before marriage will resurface deep down in the marriage life and start to trouble and haunt the marriage relationship.

The woman even during marriage must clearly know who she got married to, and the man must know who he took into marriage. If this area is not cleared and remains with grey patches during marriage, there might be a disaster and embarrassment lying ahead. Grey areas such as this do not belong in the marriage because they will cause unwanted fights between the couple. They will also affect the immediate family members as well as the extended family members on both sides of the marriage later on.

Each spouse should fully confide to the other without a shadow of doubt. The example being a question like, "Is there an area in your marriage life where you do not trust your partner fully?" This kind of question should be answered with an absolute yes, if in your mind there is something that you are still struggling to trust your partner on, such as money matters if that be the case. ***Each partner should appreciate the openness of the other, and be willing to talk about the issues causing doubt between them. Having a trustworthy relationship with your spouse brings about peace of mind and happiness.***

In the absence of trust, the love becomes very fragile between the partners. ***It is just a matter of time before love breaks down just after trust.***

Jesus said, "*Father forgive them for they know not what they do*". Those who were crucifying Him thought they fully knew what they were doing by killing Him. In actual fact, when someone does something, one thinks he or she fully knows what one is doing. When we get into relationships, especially marriage relationships, we think we fully know what we are doing. In my opinion, if that was always really the case, then 5 out of every 10 first time marriages would not end in divorce as the USA and South African statistics show. May the Lord God have mercy, big mercy for our marriage relationships.

A human being is a *"dynamic creature"* that is not static but changes with time. As the person ages he or she goes through the process of behavioral transformation, no one remains the same but only God. He is the same yesterday, today and forever. He is not a man that He should lie. For it is impossible for God to lie. So, we can fully confide and whole-heartedly trust in His ***trustworthiness***.

In one of our dialogue sessions with my wife, she made a statement that got my mind spinning for a while, such that even after the session I continued thinking about it. We were talking about trust and trusting each other in our marriage relationship. She said, *"God told me not just to trust you but I must trust Him in you".* She also mentioned that, that rested and sealed her case about trust in our relationship as a Christian couple.

In subsequent sessions we further unpacked her statement and the crux of the matter was that; as long as she thinks God is on the throne in my heart, she remains happy. However, if God is not in control of my life; then anything else to the contrary is possible and that would be scary and very threatening in our relationship. After analyzing her statement, I concluded she meant that I would be ungodly without God in my life. Then I said to her, *"It's a draw 1-1".* I said that because I chose to adopt the same attitude about trust in our marriage relationship. I saw this as the base camp and common ground where we would start to find a solution when something has gone wrong concerning trust in our marriage relationship.

There is a general understanding that when you trust your partner, you imply that you feel comfortable, safe and secured to have him or her in your life. There is also a strong aspect of reliability that you associate that partner with. The reality is that, in a relationship trust starts from the weakest point and grows to maturity. ***Trust stabilizes the marriage relationship and minimizes the chances of betrayal.*** Trust is also a process, both partners should participate in it because they are learning to trust each other, it cannot just happen in a twinkling of an eye. In other words, you should be conditioning your minds to trust each other.

In a relationship, when you mention trust you cannot finish without touching emotion, and when emotion is touched you can't go ahead without involving intimacy. This is a crucial cycle, I mean trust is also an emotion that affects intimacy. Psychologists state that trust is an emotional state of the mind and not just an expectation of behavior. It is also said by behavioral researchers that trust is a central part of all human relationships which include the following;

- Business activities and dealings
- Family life
- Medical practices
- Romantic/Intimate partnerships
- Politics

Some studies mention that trust is a feeling that somebody or something can be relied upon, or will turn out to be good. It is also said to be the feeling of being sure about something, even if it cannot be proved.

All of us know that trust is built, it can also be broken down and trust can be lost. It takes a long time to build a huge building, but it takes less than a day to destroy it. Building trust in a relationship will take a lot of time and effort. The same goes for the rebuilding of broken or lost trust. Trust is also about admitting when you are wrong and say I am sorry, and being helpful to your partner in achieving his or her goals. That is part of building trust.

ANALOGY QUIZ: TRUST			
No.	ASSESSMENT STATEMENTS (where 10 is most likely and 5 means it needs some tender loving attention)	10	5
1.	How able and reliable am I in our agreed upon deliverables of our marriage relationship?		
2.	How able and reliable is my partner in our agreed upon deliverables of our marriage relationship?		
3.	I am open to my partner about everything in our marriage relationship without any fear.		
4.	My partner is open to me about everything in our marriage relationship without any fear.		
5.	My partner appreciates my openness and trusting heart to him or her.		
6.	I appreciate the openness and trusting heart of my partner to me.		
7.	My spouse and I are having a trustworthy marriage relationship.		
8.	My partner and I fully understand that the weakness or absence of trust in a marriage relationship, causes love to become very compromised and fragile between the partners.		
9.	To my partner I'm not a difficult person to get along with.		
10.	My partner is not a difficult person to get along with to me.		

11.	Trust is built through experience but it can be lost and both of us understand that fully.		
12.	I work hard to maintain trust in our relationship, and my partner knows it.		
13.	My partner works hard to maintain trust in our relationship, and I know it.		
14.	I have full trust in my partner.		
15.	My partner has full trust in me.		
16.	Frequency of the "mistakes" I make, has potential to break the trust.		
17.	Frequency of the "mistakes" my partner makes, has potential to break the trust.		
18.	I believe that trust is strong and can be resuscitated no matter how badly broken between marriage partners.		
19.	It is still my choice to give my partner the 2nd, 3rd, 4th, or 5th chance after trust has been broken between us.		
20.	It is still my partner's choice to give me the 2nd, 3rd, 4th, or 5th chance after trust has been broken between us.		
21.	I should not try to throw the ceramic cup on the floor to test its durability and see if it will break or not.		
22.	My partner should not try to throw the ceramic cup on the floor to test its durability and see if it will break or not.		

23.	I now know who I got married with, as far as trust is concerned.		
24.	My partner now knows who he or she got married with, as far as trust is concerned.		
25.	I feel safe with my partner and have confidence that he or she won't hurt me.		

Quiz Notes:
The quiz has 25 items, having an overall score of 250 means you are doing just fine in the *"element"* as far as the 25 items are concerned; and there is minimal enhancement or improvement to be done. A score of 220 (88%) means tender loving attention is required on all items with a score of 5. A score of 200 (80%) and below means that quite a bit of work has to be done, because 20% or more of the items have scored 5 points each instead of 10. One may not comfortably say they have comfortably internalized Trust element in their relationship.

One has to do some serious introspection, and then further engage in a meaningful dialogue with the spouse about this. If things seem to be overwhelming, you still have the professional counselor on your side for guidance. Remember, the quiz is not the counselor, it only gives clues as to say, among others, what things you need to consider in your endeavor of improving Trust in your relationship.

CHAPTER 3

COMMITMENT

The general understanding is that every person who got into marriage had a choice to marry or remain single, so they decided to commit themselves to marriage. So each spouse has a duty to see to it that the other spouse is happy. Listen to what the wise master builder Apostle Paul said;

"[33]But ***a married man*** has to think about ***his earthly responsibilities*** and how ***to please his wife.*** [34]His interests are divided. In the same way, a woman who is no longer married or has never been married can be devoted to the Lord and holy in body and in spirit. But ***a married woman*** has to think about ***her earthly responsibilities*** and how ***to please her husband.***"
(1 Cor. 7:33-34 NLT).

It cannot be over-emphasized that the married couple has a duty to commit to work on their marriage relationship. ***The critical part of the marriage union is the relationship which exists between the couple.*** The nature of that relationship whether it is good or bad is greatly influenced by the abundance or lack of the elements of a good and happy marriage as discussed in a number of chapters in this book. ***When you are committed and invested in the marriage relationship, you are more likely to remain true even in the presence of attractive and tempting alternatives around you. I say so because commitment is stronger than cheating on your partner, one will not cheat and lie if he or she has a strong commitment to the marriage relationship.***

However, if the commitment is not there, then cheating will take its toll. Here is another interesting passage by my all-time role model;

28 "But what do you think about this? A man with two sons told the older son, 'Son, go out and work in the vineyard today.'
29 The son answered, 'No, I won't go,' but later he changed his mind and went anyway.
30 Then the father told the other son, 'You go,' and he said, 'Yes, sir, I will.' But he didn't go.
31 "Which of the two obeyed his father?" They replied, "The first."

Then Jesus explained His meaning: "I tell you the truth, corrupt tax collectors and prostitutes will get into the Kingdom of God before you do.
32 For John the Baptist came and showed you the right way to live, but you didn't believe him, while tax collectors and prostitutes did. And even when you saw this happening, you refused to believe him and repent of your sins."
(Matt. 21:28-32 NLT).

Commitment, if you have it, will always make you have the second thought when you initially decide not to do what you ought to do. Let it be your principle in life, always commit to do what is right for you to do in all circumstances. Committed partners will never let each other down willfully and they never get weary of supporting one another. However, where there is no mutual commitment, even the committed partner may perhaps see no point of cooking for the uncommitted partner; because he or she would eventually die of hunger as that partner would even be lazy to wake up and dish for himself or herself. The analogy here is that, the whole effort of cooking would be useless or wasted effort if the food will not be eaten after all, as far as the partner who cooked is concerned.

The ideal situation would be; as commitment makes one partner to cook before leaving for work, commitment will also make one partner to wake up and dish for himself and then wash the dishes after eating. Commitment is more than just saying, *"We want to live under the same roof as love partners."* It also means choosing to stick with one another as long as you live, that means for life regardless of difficult moments. Commitment means casting all doubts and being sold out wholeheartedly to the marriage relationship, and working it out to make it work for the two of you. This also refers to not giving up on each other, where each partner gives out his or her own best for the benefit of the other partner.

Some studies reveal that commitment in marriage means you do what it takes to make the relationship successful. As a couple it is your choice to start and build a committed marriage relationship, what I mean is that it is up to the people of the marriage to commit to their relationship. ***You should appreciate your partner's commitment as soon as you see it.*** Say it to the detail as you see it, and it will have a meaningful impact to your partner, and that will strengthen his or her commitment even further. The most important type of commitment for couples should be the commitment to their marriages.

Commitment is not an event but rather an ongoing process, it is crucial to choose to work on it on a continuous basis as a couple.

ANALOGY QUIZ: COMMITMENT			
No.	ASSESSMENT STATEMENTS (where 10 is most likely and 5 means it needs some tender loving attention)	10	5
1.	It is part of my duties to see to it that my partner is happy in our marriage relationship.		
2.	It is part of my partner's duties to see to it that I am happy in our marriage relationship.		
3.	I have made it part of my life to commit to work daily on our marriage relationship.		
4.	I have and will remain committed to my marriage relationship in the presence of attractive and tempting alternatives.		
5.	I am aware of what my partner is doing daily to work on our relationship to be better.		
6.	My partner is fully aware of what I am doing daily to work on our relationship to be better.		
7.	I am very much appreciative of my partner's commitment to our relationship.		
8.	My partner is very much appreciative of my commitment to our relationship.		
9.	We are committed marriage partners who never let each other down willfully.		
10.	It is in our continuous plans to always strengthen our marriage commitment.		

11.	We spend enough time reviewing and talking about our marriage commitment.		
12.	Deeper analysis of marriage commitment has brought us closer as a couple.		

Quiz Notes:
The quiz has 12 items, having an overall score of 120 means you are doing just fine in this *"element"* as far as the 12 items are concerned; and there is minimal enhancement or improvement needed. A score below 120-100 (85%) means tender loving attention is required on all items that score a 5. A score of 60 (50%) and below means that one has to do a lot of work to reach confidence level on this *"element"*. One has to do some serious introspection, and then further engage in a meaningful dialogue with the spouse. If things seem to be overwhelming, you still have the professional counselor on your side for guidance. Remember, the quiz is not the counselor, it only gives clues as to say, among others, what things you need to consider on your way to making your marriage good and happy as far as the element of Commitment is concerned.

CHAPTER 4

MAKING TIME, PAYING ATTENTION & HAVING FUN

MAKING TIME

Greater improvement in the marriage relationship quality, happens over a period of time and is not instant. ***Making time and taking time to work on your relationship will yield good dividends over a period of time.*** Value the time and the time will give you its value. It is a researched fact that marriages get less happy over a period of time. That is why we hear people separate after many years of being married together.

When compared to rhino poaching that is happening in South Africa, more rhino's stand a better chance of surviving than most marriages. I say this because at least something serious is being done to stop the poaching. However, it seems to be free for all when it comes to marriage life destruction. I am of the view that not enough effort is being done to save marriages, especially by the people of the marriage themselves.

We can make our marriage unions happy and better by allowing time to give its value to our marriage relationships. Everybody makes mistakes and your spouse will make mistakes too, even more often than you would imagine. So, the issue of making mistakes shouldn't be the fuss here. However, the mistakes that we make should improve over time, and each spouse should work on that so that the other spouse notices the improvement. Sometimes it is not easy for the other partner to see the improvement and that is where dialogue comes handy. It gives you a chance to state your case, and explain yourself to your partner as to where you have improved and how.

It can happen over a period of time for one to achieve the desired behavioral change, and that would be perfect for the relationship to be a happy one. ***Do not rush it and force it on each other, value the time and the time will give its value to your relationship. Don't win more than what you cannot afford to lose.*** What I mean is that, in your endeavor of working hard chasing your career goals and making a living for your family; don't gain that and lose your family in part if not the whole of it in the process.

Let me go another step further, if the *"winning"* of one spouse means the *"losing"* to the other spouse every time, that causes an agitation to the losing spouse and that agitation is very toxic to the marriage relationship. It has to be a *"win-win"* situation for most of the times. Some social psychologists and researchers subscribe to the view that no relationship between couples is 100% equal. Which means that one partner will love more than the other. They also allude to the fact that the partner who loves a bit more, is always at the greater risk of being hurt more when things go wrong in the relationship. Making quality time with one another will assist the couples to successfully deal with the love imbalances in the relationship amicably, in a friendly and peaceable manner so to speak.

Making quality time is very important in a marriage relationship, because quality time together is also a great way of building your friendship with your partner. You should constantly aim to always remain best friends with your spouse, and best friends always keep the connection intact and alive. ***The quality time experience helps to create closeness and exclusivity in the couple's relationship, it also enhances better understanding of each other's thinking and feelings.***

Bear in mind, ***nothing in the couples' relationship will change for the better until the couples do.*** Making time might just do the trick and turn things around in your marriage relationship. Don't make a mistake by ranking this element low, it might just surprise you because it can make the thing that matters matter in your marriage. Another thing that is a big enemy to making quality time is the smartphone addiction to one or both spouses. This gadget has taken over most of our every day's time as married couples, and the marriage relationships are suffering as a result.

Couples are spending more that time with their smartphones than spending time with each other, and still expect their marriage relationships to be among the best. ***This kind of addiction also raises toxicity levels in the relationship.*** Couples have to apply a good time management in order to control their cyber space attention. Making time for one another should not be overtaken by smartphone addiction.

Please understand me correctly, I'm not demonizing smartphones and their usage, but that should be done ethically as far as the marriage relationship is concerned. Some spouses have given up to the reality that our lives are controlled and centered around the smartphones, because they are with us wherever we go. However, that has to change if we want our marriage relationships to be healthy, strong and happy.

The fact of the matter is that our marriage relationships are seriously competing over quality time with the smartphone addiction, and guess who always wins. The answer is the obvious smartphone excessive usage and that has to be turned around and managed. It is sad to hear couples saying, *"The smartphone addiction has taken over our quality time and it is controlling it."* So, it is now high time for this to be put under control if couples really want healthy, strong and happy marriage relationships.

Perhaps I would also imagine on this one, that in most cases it's a matter of winning battles here and there but the war will still be on; but never give up on trying to do the right thing rather than doing nothing at all. I understand that this challenge is not limited to smartphones, there are others like watching television, the emphasis is on smartphones because they take the biggest chunk due to the fact they are always with us wherever we go. This interactive engagement happens indoors and outdoors, and even when we are airborne in airplanes sitting next to each other, what a pity.

The quality time with your partner is all about mindfully spending time together in order to show your appreciation and affection for one another, and also to improve the connection and intimacy in the relationship. It means not just sitting in the same room at the same time and each one doing his or her own thing, but it means actively choosing to make time for each other and for the relationship.

ANALOGY QUIZ: MAKING TIME			
No.	**ASSESSMENT STATEMENTS** (where 10 is most likely and 5 means it needs some tender loving attention)	**10**	**5**
1.	Over a period of time the quality of our marriage relationship has improved greatly instead of regressing.		
2.	We value time in the relationship as a couple, and by doing that we believe that time will give its value to our relationship.		
3.	The mistakes that we make in our relationship have improved over a period of time.		
4.	In our relationship, we give each other time to self-correct because no one is faultless and perfect.		
5.	Over a period of time I have noticed my behavior changing for the better.		
6.	Over a period of time I have noticed my partner's behavior changing for the better.		
7.	I do not rush and force behavioral change on my partner, I allow time to have its course.		
8.	My partner does not rush or force behavioral change on me, he or she allows time to have its course.		
9.	I agree with the fact that marriages get less happy over a period of time, and I can do something positive about that.		
10.	I easily see improvement in my mistakes.		

11.	I easily see improvement in my partner's mistakes.		
12.	We are giving enough time to save our marriage relationship from deteriorating and becoming toxic.		
13.	In most instances when I win, it means that my partner is also winning.		
14.	In most instances when my partner wins, it means that I am also winning.		
15.	My partner and I are always best friends who keep connection intact and alive.		
16.	We fully understand that nothing will change for the better in our relationship until we do.		
17.	My smartphone usage or addiction is now under control.		
18.	My partner's smartphone usage or addiction is now under control.		
19.	Our quality time has not been overtaken by smartphone addiction.		
20.	My emotions are not agitated by my partner's overuse of smartphone.		
21.	My partner's emotions are not agitated by my overuse of smartphone.		
22.	Cyber space attention by either spouse is not causing commotion in our relationship, because we fought against the smartphone addiction and won.		

Quiz Notes:

The quiz has 22 items, having an overall score of 220 means that you are doing just fine in the *"element"* as far as the 22 items are concerned; and there is minimal enhancement or improvement that needs to be done. A score of 198 (90%) means tender loving attention is required on all items with a score of 5. A score of 165 (75%) and below means that quite a bit of work has to be done, because 25% or more of the items have scored 5 points each instead of 10. One may not comfortably say they have mastered and internalized the Making of Time in their relationship.

One has to do some serious introspection, and then further engage in a meaningful dialogue with the spouse about this. If things seem to be overwhelming, you still have the professional counselor on your side for guidance. Remember, the quiz is not the counselor, it only gives clues as to say, among others, what things you need to consider in your endeavor of improving Making Time for your relationship.

PAYING ATTENTION

Having looked at Wikipedia for definitions, I deduce from what I got and say that, attention is the behavioral and cognitive process of selectively concentrating on a specific person, while ignoring other people that are also present in your space. Attention means among other things, taking notice of your spouse and at the same time regarding him or her as an interesting and important person in your life. You have to make sure that he or she is able to hear and see you doing it. ***Always avoid saying hurtful things to your partner, because that provokes an undesirable attention.***

The behavioral researchers state that attention plays a critical role in almost every area of life including learning, work, and relationships. To keep the marriage lamp trimmed and clear, it needs positive attention from both partners. We are a very busy generation juggling around a lot of modern time demands of life. Happy couples do make time for each other. You cannot be a workaholic such that you have no time for your immediate family with the pretense that you are working very hard for them and their future.

That might be a false pretense that actually works against your marriage relationship. Indeed, work is very important but one must learn to keep the balance such that the relationship will not suffer. The better way is to talk about your busy schedules and lifestyle as a couple; then each partner has to come up with suggestions as how to strike a balance for the benefit of the relationship. Try your suggested options together, and you will be amazed as to how you will flow in navigating the maze of life happily together with less hassles in the midst of your busy lifestyle.

Some common studies of the practical gestures of attention towards your partner suggest the following:

- Being mindful rather than forgetful of birthdays, and surprise your partner with something special no matter how small it is.

- You can make verbal affirmations saying you care so much that you want him or her, to be successful in every positive aspect of life.

- As the token of appreciation for doing good to you in one way or the other, you can take your partner to some favorite dining places as and when convenient to both of you.

- Some studies suggest that you can do ***"that thing"*** your partner always wanted you to do but never got time to do it. (e.g. taking a break and go on that most wanted and promised holiday trip).

- Giving out a budget or ***"blank cheque"*** by letting the partner choose what he or she wants to do this coming weekend with it. (It could be hairstyle change; pair of new shoes or sneakers, a visit to the game reserve, etc.).

What I mean is that, show some interest in your partner's life, provide the needed support and show that you care so much. It is said that, ***"No one cares how much you know until they know how much you care".*** Always make time to give that undivided attention to your spouse, remember he or she is the love of your life and wants to see you demonstrating it and hear you saying it.

Attention supports the maintenance of good communication in the relationship. When a partner ignores the other instead of giving attention, that can put the relationship in an undesirable situation. This can be very depressing to the partner who feels ignored. I also concur with the view that this has some diminishing effects to the sufferer's confidence and purpose about life. He or she may feel like a nuisance in the relationship, meaning that the partner feels like an inconvenience to the other partner to be in the relationship. Whereas, on the other hand, ***an attentive partner pumps happiness into the other partner's life.***

"[22]But *Samuel declared: "Does the LORD delight in burnt offerings and sacrifices as much as in obedience to His voice? Behold, obedience is better than sacrifice, and attentiveness is better than the fat of rams."*
(1 Sam 15:22-23).

ANALOGY QUIZ: PAYING ATTENTION			
No.	**ASSESSMENT STATEMENTS** (where 10 is most likely and 5 means it needs some tender loving attention)	**10**	**5**
1.	I have the ability to give attention to my partner and our relationship in the midst of other important people in my space.		
2.	My partner has the ability to give attention to me and our relationship in the midst of other important people in his or her space.		
3.	On numerous occasions I have seen my partner giving me the much needed attention when it mattered most.		
4.	On numerous occasions my partner has seen me giving to him or her the much needed attention when it mattered most.		
5.	I regard my spouse as the most special and important person in my life and he or she knows it.		
6.	My spouse regards me as the most special and important person in his or her life and I know it.		
7.	I have the ability not to provoke an undesirable attention from my partner.		
8.	My partner has the ability not to provoke an undesirable attention from me.		
9.	In our busy schedule of our daily lifestyle, my partner and I know how to strike a balance for the benefit of our marriage relationship.		

10.	We have discovered what to do to get each other's attention when it is lacking.		

Quiz Notes:
The quiz has 10 items, and having an overall score of 100 means you are doing just fine in this *"element"* as far as the 10 items are concerned, and there is minimal enhancement or improvement that needs to be done. A score below 100-80 (80%) means tender loving attention is required on all items that score a 5. A score of 50 (50%) and below means that one has to do a lot of work to reach the confidence level on this *"element"*. One has to do some serious introspection, and then further engage in a meaningful dialogue with the spouse. If things seem to be overwhelming, you still have the professional counselor on your side for guidance. Remember, the quiz is not the counselor, it only gives clues as to say, among others, what things you need to consider on your way to making your marriage happy as far as the element of Attention is concerned.

HAVING FUN

Well, now that we are adults, what does it mean to have fun or to play?

A broad definition of play is, "any pleasurable use of discretionary time."
(Charles, 1983).

Colarusso, 1993 further states that, ***"What is pleasurable may of course, vary from person to person."*** He also alludes that researchers have discovered that play is not only pleasurable, but also serves as a developmental activity; as in children when they learn and develop through play, play can also promote the engagement and mastery of developmental tasks in adults.

So, agree with your partner that through play and having fun, you want to contribute to your marriage to be one of the best and happy marriages ever lived by couples; and having fun is part of the contribution towards that goal. Keep on keeping on, don't be weary and stop. Keep doing the right things for your marriage. I have learnt that some people take the mystery of the marriage union for granted after some notable years in marriage. One must be prepared to encounter some interesting discoveries about his or her partner as this mystery unfolds. Each partner must be flexible to discover and learn new things about the other partner every day as long as they live. Yes, I agree, the marriage relationship shouldn't be boring, dull and tedious.

According to the philosophy of Plato the Greek philosopher, he states that, ***"You can discover more about a person in an hour of play than in a year of conversation."*** It is true that people can oftentimes mask their true selves while talking in conversation. However, play is a form of modeling real life, which brings forth true reactions to different circumstances. It is a fact that play can teach us about ourselves and our partners, based on how we all react in various situations facing us during the time of play. The researched realistic example is that, what a person does to overcome a difficult situation during play, will likely be the same way he or she would overcome difficult situations in real life.

The human being is never static but a dynamic creature. The secret is to learn together about each other in the marriage relationship. So, have fun discovering new things about each other and live your lives happily. Live and let live, I mean live your life and the let your partner live his or her life too, and allow no selfishness or intolerance to stand in the way of fun.

The review of literature below alludes to the element of having fun through play:

"Having fun together helps couples feel positive emotions, which can increase relationship satisfaction, help couples to unite in order to overcome differences and give hope when working through difficult challenges."
(Aune & Wong, 2002; Betcher, 1977; Lauer & Lauer, 2002).

"When couples first meet they usually spend a significant amount of time engaging in fun activities together, and spending quality time getting to know each other. A majority of people would probably plan to keep that fun and spark continuing in their relationship, but over time with all the household chores, kids, meetings, long work hours, and everyday challenges; taking time to really enjoy being together and have fun often takes a back seat to other priorities."
(Markman, Stanley, Blumberg, Jenkins & Whiteley, 2004: Parrott & Parrott, 2006).

While the effort of having fun by being playful is enjoyable in relationships, the playing as couples is not only about having fun, but it can also serve other beneficial functions in the marriage relationship.

"Play can also promote spontaneity when life seems routine, serve as a reminder of positive relationship history, and promote intimacy."
(Baxter, 1992; Lauer & Lauer, 2002).

There is also a great possibility of enhancing both emotional and physical health by having fun. Don't deprive yourselves by saying, *"We are old now and we should not waste time by playing, we are not children anymore."*

"Some studies have even discovered that having fun together is the most important factor in the sense of friendship, commitment, and the greatest influence on overall marital satisfaction."
(Markman, et al., 2004).

There are common limitations that couples have to overcome on their way to having fun in their relationships. You may wish to brainstorm a list of activities you would like to try that you think would be fun for you as a couple to do. Prioritize them, take a calendar and allocate possible dates and you may even allocate some financial resources where necessary in order to make this possible.

The couples have to be willing, flexible and committed to their plans and actions among other things for them to be effective in this element. Having fun in the marriage relationship should not be accidental or by chance, it should be intentional and coming from both partners amicably. The barriers will come but the partners will need to make plans all the time in order to overcome them. ***Strong, happy and long lasting marriage relationships do not just happen but they require time and effort of working smart.*** So, be ready to commit time, effort and smartness to having fun together with your partner.

What is fun to one couple would not necessarily be fun for other couples. However, the smartness of couples will make them derive fun when they see each other enjoying the togetherness and companionship. Seeing your partner enjoying the enjoyment of playing together creates fun, and one would like to repeat that enjoyable moment again and again.

Don't be what you are not, just remain who you are all the way. Do not live a life of a fake somebody but be realistic and live a life of who you are; and you will enjoy life and please enjoy it to the fullest.

ANALOGY QUIZ: HAVING FUN			
No.	ASSESSMENT STATEMENTS (where 10 is most likely and 5 means it needs some tender loving attention)	10	5
1.	I make time to have fun in our marriage relationship.		
2.	My partner makes time to have fun in our marriage relationship.		
3.	We make plans and take actions and time to enjoy our companionship as a couple.		
4.	I enjoy seeing my partner enjoying the enjoyment of playing together.		
5.	My partner enjoys seeing myself enjoying the enjoyment of playing together.		
6.	Enjoyment of playing together creates fun, and I would like to repeat that enjoyment again and again.		
7.	Enjoyment of playing together creates fun, and my partner would like to repeat that enjoyment again and again.		
8.	My partner has the ability not to We're not a fake couple, we live a life of who we are, and we're living our life enjoyably to the fullest.		
9.	We understand that what is fun to other couples would not necessarily be fun for us. So we can't be copycats, we always do what suits us as a couple.		

10.	Togetherness and companionship are given a boost when we are having fun.		
11.	Our willingness, flexibility, plan and commitment work wonders in materializing our fun.		
12.	I agree with the fact that we are never too old to play and have fun as a couple.		

Quiz Notes:
The quiz has 12 items, having an overall score of 120 means you are doing just fine in the *"element"* as far as the 12 items are concerned; and there is minimal enhancement or improvement that needs to be done. A score of 100 (83%) means tender loving attention is required on all items with a score of 5. A score of 85 (70%) and below means that quite a bit of work has to be done, because 30% or more of the items have scored 5 points each instead of 10. One may not comfortably say they have mastered or internalized Having Fun in their relationship.

So, one has to do some serious introspection, and then further engage in a meaningful dialogue with the spouse about this. If things seem to be overwhelming, you still have the professional counselor on your side for guidance. Remember, the quiz is not the counselor, it only gives clues as to say, among others, what things you need to consider in your endeavor of improving Having Fun in the relationship.

CHAPTER 5

GOOD COMMUNICATION & LISTENING

When it comes to communication definitions, the Merriam-Webster dictionary gives me one of the best. It defines communication as the act or process of using words, sounds, signs, or behaviors to express or exchange information or to express your ideas, thoughts, feelings, etc., to someone else.

Whereas, the Oxford languages dictionary brings a powerful, clear and flowing definition when they define listening by saying that, "Listening is receiving language through the ears, listening involves identifying the sounds of speech and processing them into words and sentences." Listening in any language requires focus and attention. It is a skill that some people need to work on, harder than others.

Communication is also about presenting, conveying and imparting a message of some kind to the intended receiver. This is done with the expectation that it will be understood the same way the sender understands it. That is not always the case, which is what complicates the subject of communication especially in relationships. There is also another element which is crucial in the process which is called listening, this plays a big role in the hearing and interpretation of the message. I have paired these two together for the purpose of their brief discussion.

It is factual that communicating about positive events in your marriage boosts mental health and positive emotions beyond the actual events themselves. This further enhances better bonding in the relationship, so the couple should focus more on the therapeutic style of communication. I mean communications that has healing effects to both parties, sender and the receiver.

When you see or feel something, you need to say something about it to your spouse. ***Verbalize what you think, verbalize what you feel and verbalize what you see. Revive the dialogue and it works for the relationship.*** If the marriage relationship has gone sideways, the power of dialogue will help to put it back on track. I mean a ***constructive discussion intended to solve a problem, and that is what a dialogue is all about.*** It will surely make a meaningful contribution to your marriage relationship.

When it comes to communication, you need to establish a pattern that works well for both of you. The crux of the matter here is that both of you should understand it for it to work for you, or else you will always find yourselves not singing from the same hymnbook. You should know how he or she reacts to disappointment, failure, discouragement and anger. You also need to know how he or she acts when happy, prospering, succeeding, moneyed and joyful.

Communication is the artery or the blood vein of the marriage relationship. There might be a number of life's challenges that will try and block the blood-flow in this vein, and if it means you have to do a by-pass for your communication to make it work, do it. Sometimes it may need a triple by-pass or more, please do it for the sake of saving your marriage relationship. I hope you get me on this one.

Lack of communication is the number one cause of divorce in South Africa followed by money matters. (Statistics South Africa, 2018).

This means that South African marriage relationships are under tremendous pressure due to poor and toxic communication in prevalence amongst couples.

For every voice there's got to be an ear to listen or the voice's message will be useless effort. How many times have you sent an electronic message to your partner and discovered that it was read on the second day? If never, lucky you. It means that your partner gives high priority to all messages coming from you and will take the necessary action timeously. This is highly beneficial to effectuate a healthy relationship in the marriage. When the communication is poor the other partner may even feel that the other partner is not taking him or her seriously, whereas, it may not necessarily be the case.

When in conversation with your partner about a specific issue and you seem not to be in agreement as both of you are sticking to your guns, ***you should remember that it's not always about being right but it's about reaching an amicable solution as a couple.*** If that doesn't happen you'll be getting to nowhere. The more you try to convince your partner that you are right and his or her opinion is wrong, you will be making them worse as if you are reinforcing what they believe to be right. Therefore, you may not succeed in getting your spouse to change the mind.

Perhaps you should try to find a common ground with your partner by putting yourself into his or her shoes so to speak. Then you will be on the same page together looking at the same challenge from the same angle and perspective. I suppose from that angle you'll be able to find an amicable solution. Applying the skill of ***"listening to understand"*** rather than ***"listening to respond"*** will also help a great deal towards getting to a solution that will be acceptable to both of you.

Otherwise trying to change your partner's belief to that of yours may not assist in coming to a win-win solution. I would say that the first thing to do is to stop resisting and being defensive, just be easy and take it easy and then get into your partner's shoes. Then again, both of you will be next to each other looking at the problem instead of facing each other with hot words of confrontation.

One other sign that the communication is not good is that of a tense relationship in the marriage, and this may be due to a number of toxins at play such as resentment, active enmity, acrimony, betrayal, bitterness, etc.

It helps a lot to be realistic and face the facts. Find out what do you want, do you want to be right or do you want to get to an amicable solution regarding the point of disagreement with your spouse? You might have already found out by now that when you try to argue to change your husband or wife to see and believe things the way you do; you are actually making him or her to be a bit stubborn than before and to hold his or her own view even the more.

Common studies reveal that you judge the meaning and effectiveness of your communication by the response you get from your spouse. He or she should also judge the meaning and the effectiveness of his or her communication by the response he or she gets from you. Perhaps the same should apply when it comes to our children and so forth. That is why it is important to be flexible in order to be effective and be understood by your partner. ***Always pursue a non-violent***

way of communication. Shouting at your partner will not change anything to your liking, not anytime soon.

What do you do when you two have an impasse and no one wants to talk to the other thereafter? Again, you might want to jump into your partner's shoes and re-open the conversation differently, at this time try to understand what your partner meant to say in the first place. The partner might be willing to re-explain himself or herself, when that happens don't allow things to mess up again. Now try to listen to understand and not to be defensive defending your own point of view before even understanding the viewpoint of your partner fully. I wish you success in all your retries, but to be honest with you, it works.

Remember that the outcome of your communication is very important, and if most of the time it is not good, it is high time that you work seriously on your communication skills. Poor communication also means that there's an imbalance between the partners. You need to learn to do things together harmoniously and by agreement.

"Do two walk together unless they have agreed to do so?" (Amos 3:3 NIV).

The fact of the matter is that as a human being you are perfectly imperfect, even as a couple you are just like wise. As partners you need to work on things that build each other's self-esteem and indirectly, you will be boosting each other's self-worth in the relationship. You should not fail to understand that each partner has his or her own subjective opinions about life, which you still need to talk about and understand. That is one of the reasons why your partner behaves the way he or she does and you also do things differently. By adopting the principle of healthy dialogue you will make it easy for yourselves to find each other on various matters concerning your relationship.

Another crucial point is that you need to share each other's standards, principles and values. I want to assure you, that kind of dialogue will bring you closer and closer to the personality of your partner. It is one way of bringing a portion of the inner heart out. This should enhance to you the principle of teaching each other about each other. Establish a communication pattern that works well for both of you. When that process is functional, it will assist you as a couple to deal with the bad *"Stonewalling"* which promotes disengagement from all forms of meaningful conversation.

You should remember to understand that, during your dialogue there will be issues that you will not reach consensus on for the first, second or even third time. Yes, there will be issues where you don't seem to have agreeable alternatives. Perhaps it may be time when the third party advice may come handy, if you can't reboot and start over again. Bear in mind, there are those who have walked this road before, it may be worth a while to listen to them. Obviously, it does not mean that you must take the alternative solutions suggested by a third party, but by listening to their suggested solutions; you might be able as a couple to work out your own agreeable solutions better than before.

There's no *"one size fits all"* type of solution in marriage relationships, and ***each couple is uniquely unique.*** Hence I stated that, it is important as a couple to ***understand what makes the unique you uniquely you.***

Another area that mars and scars communication is that of being overly independent. When one partner is too independent, it might cause a problem for the other. ***What I mean is that one***

partner thinks, decides and implements things as if the other partner does not exist. Bear in mind that you are no longer living a life of your own alone, it is now a shared life with your partner as long as you live. The execution of some decisions without the knowledge of the other spouse might start a friction which could have been avoided. The fact of the matter is that you are no longer a single, you're now a married person.

In life I have found the human being to be a very dynamic creature, and that has caused him or her to be unstable by nature, to put it simple, the older the grumpier and the more it becomes very difficult to deal with. However, I said it already, take it easy with each other as partners. May be my voice is too low, let me be loud and clear; "DO NOT DEAL WITH THE NOT SO GOOD ISSUES ABOUT YOUR PARTNER IN THE CONTEMPT THAT THEY BREED!" The crux of the matter is that he or she is your best friend, love of your life, helpmate and not your enemy or attacker. So, do not attack your partner by blaming, insulting and even by raising your voice and shouting at him or her on any issue. Obviously, unless the house is on fire.

I've found this element of communication and listening very difficult to master because of the dynamic nature of partners in relationships. Sometimes it is just like aiming for a rapidly moving target, you have to miss it a few times before you can think you've hit it. Then, it raises up again as something else and you have to start aiming at it again. So, this one can give you a real ***"run-around"*** emotionally speaking, and many couples did not manage to keep up with that and they failed their marriage as a result. This has been the case in South Africa because the lack of communication is currently rated as number one cause of all divorces in the country.
(Stats SA, 2018).

ANALOGY QUIZ: GOOD COMMUNICATION & LISTENING			
No.	**ASSESSMENT STATEMENTS** (where 10 is most likely and 5 means it needs some tender loving attention)	**10**	**5**
1.	Communication and listening are at a good & satisfactory level in our marriage relationship.		
2.	My partner and I are very much conscious of therapeutic communication in our marriage relationship.		
3.	I often communicate to my partner what I think, see and feel about our marriage relationship.		
4.	My partner often communicates to me what he or she thinks, sees and feels about our marriage relationship.		
5.	I always listen to understand rather than listen to respond when my partner talks to me.		
6.	My partner always listens to understand rather than listen to respond when I talk to him or her.		
7.	Constructive and successful dialogue is at its best level ever in our relationship.		
8.	I always inform my partner about any of my actions that may result in our marriage relationship being affected negatively by the results thereof.		

9.	My partner always inform me about any of his or her actions that may result in our marriage relationship being affected negatively by the results thereof.		
10.	I have a feeling that my partner is taking me seriously when it comes to communication & listening.		
11.	I reckon my partner has a feeling that I take him or her seriously when it comes to communication & listening.		
12.	Communication with my partner is still nice and good like it enjoyably used to be many years back.		
13.	I am a good and patient listener in our relationship.		
14.	My partner is a good and patient listener in our relationship.		
15.	Even when I am annoyed I do not talk when my partner is still talking.		
16.	My partner does not talk when I am still talking even when he or she is annoyed.		
17.	I never raise my voice or shout at my partner in rage unless he or she is about to get hurt.		
18.	My partner never raises voice or shouts at me in rage unless I am about to get hurt.		
19.	Often times I try to convince my partner not to take my view when we are not in agreement but I would take his or hers.		

20.	Often times my partner would be flexible to take my view when we are not in agreement.		
21.	I have made peace with the fact that, as far as decision making is concerned, I'm no longer living a life of my own alone, it is now a shared life with my partner as long as we live.		
22.	My partner has made peace with the fact that, as far as decision making is concerned, he/she is no longer living a life of his/her own alone, it is now a shared life as long as we live.		
23.	We always find the element of communication & listening easy to deal with in our relationship.		
24.	I agree to the fact that I'm perfectly imperfect, including our relationship.		
25.	I like it, and enjoy engaging in a healthy dialogue with my partner.		

Quiz Notes:
The quiz has 25 items, having an overall score of 250 means you are doing just fine in the *"element"* as far as the 25 items are concerned; and there is minimal enhancement or improvement that needs to be done. A score of 220 (88%) means tender loving attention is required on all items with a score of 5. A score of 200 (80%) and below means that quite a bit of work has to be done, because 20% or more of the items have scored 5 points each instead of 10. One may not comfortably say they have mastered or internalized Communication & Listening in their relationship.

One has to do some serious introspection, and then further engage in a meaningful dialogue with the spouse about this. If things seem to be overwhelming, you still have the professional counselor on your side for guidance. Remember, the quiz is not the counselor, it only gives clues as to say, among others, what things you need to consider in your endeavor of improving Communication & Listening in your relationship.

CHAPTER 6

PARTNERSHIP & DOING THINGS TOGETHER

PARTNERSHIP

There ***is beauty in the power of the diversified talents of married couples*** when it comes to the management of family projects, let me rather call them family events and occasions. The talents and capabilities of one spouse start to manifest and blend beautifully; and they wonderfully complement those of other spouse. I just admire to watch this happening, not just from my own family but from other families as well.

Diversity in marriage is just a beauty, the couple has to nurture and cherish it and that also strengthens the partnership in the relationship. There's a saying which says, *"None of us is as good as all of us."* Always learn to work as members of one team that are not competing with one another but complementing each other. I always admire and wonder at the human eyes coordination, although they are two but they always work together. It is not possible for one eye to look down when the other is looking up. When it's time to rest and sleep both eyes will be closed, one eye cannot remain open. The fact of the matter is that both eyes like to function together always. Look at this beautiful passage;

The value of a partner:
"[9]Two are better than one,Because they have a good reward for their labor.
[10]For if they fall, one will lift up his companion.
But woe to him who is alone when he falls,
For he has no one to help him up.
[11]Again, if two lie down together, they will keep warm;
But how can one be warm alone?
[12]Though one may be overpowered by another, two can withstand him.
And a threefold cord is not quickly broken."
(Eccl. 4:9-12 NKJV).

Celebrate good times and achievements together as a couple. Becoming partners to each other is a learning process like all other elements of good and happy marriages. You need to know and understand your very own personality, work on it to be the best that it can be for the sake of pursuing a happy marriage relationship. One should be willing and prepared to do the right thing over and over again, with the aim of working their marriage relationship to be better.

One might say, ***"I just can't change my personality, I'm a cut and dried extrovert."*** That's sounds well and good, but one can change some of his or her behaviors. That is what I mean by working on your personality for pursuing a happy marriage relationship. Working on your behaviors constantly and persistently will eventually tap on your personality and make it more compatible to that of your partner, and the marriage relationship is set to benefit from that big time or to a great extent. However, this should not be one sided, this should work well with reciprocity where the other partner would do the same.

The crux of the matter is that you should actively seek ways to collaborate with your partner, because partnership is also about collaboration amongst the partners. Always work on your marriage relationship because the potential gains of that have unlimited upside. Continue making the difference no matter how small in the life of your partner. Remember that the outcomes or results of your behaviors define the shape of your personality, because not everything you do that hurts your partner is always by mistake even though you may say, ***"Honey, I'm sorry."***

Partnership in marriage means both partners can make equal contributions on all decisions in the relationship. No one is limited to only making small contributions, while the other can make big and limitless contributions. The wife is the help-mate to the husband and she has to help him in every aspect possible, without any deprivation to do so. In addition, both partners should feel that they can influence each other freely in their decision making process. This would show that there's a spirit of equality in the marriage, in the sense that no one is said to be an inferior partner than the other.

The equality in the marriage should not be confused with the undisputable fact that, the husband is always the head of the family, and the wife is part of that family. Equality in the marriage does not replace this headship, but equality recognizes the headship. The couple will not be confused by this if they understand the difference between authority and equality.

In a true partnership, both husband and wife can express themselves without fear of judgment or prejudice, they can work together towards common goals and have equal influence over important decisions to be made in the marriage relationship. The couple will also be able in a healthy manner to grow emotionally, psychologically and spiritually as a result of their happy partnership in the marriage.

When spouses in a marriage union value equality, they see each other as equals and no one is seen to be inferior or lower grade than the other. They treat each other with respect, consider each other's needs, and support one another in every aspect of their life. The fact of the matter is that, equal partners agree on goals together and work as a team to achieve these goals.

Let me briefly revisit the issue of equality in case I have caused somebody's mind to spin, perhaps I might have left someone's heart chasing two beats per second. Okay now, please cool down. Equality means the state of being equal, especially in status, rights, or opportunities. It is also associated with fairness, justness and impartiality. Again, the couple should be able to differentiate between authority and equality, which both are applicable at the same time in our marriage relationships. I trust this clears the air a little bit.

The partners in partnership indicate that they want to share their lives with one another. Some studies state that a true partnership is when you believe that your spouse will always do what is best for you even if it is not best for him or her. Another quality of a good partnership is that partners value each other's interests separate from their own, they are very supportive of one another's overall goals in life.

Listen to this beautiful passage:
"[9]Two people are better off than one, for they can help each other succeed. [10]If one person falls, the other can reach out and help. But someone who falls alone is in real trouble." (Eccl. 4:9-10 NLT).

The case of partnership arrangement is such that partners agree to cooperate to advance their mutual interests. Partnership is committing to learn to work as a team.

ANALOGY QUIZ: PARTNERSHIP			
No.	**ASSESSMENT STATEMENTS** (where 10 is most likely and 5 means it needs some tender loving attention)	**10**	**5**
1.	Diversity is a beauty and strength in our marriage relationship.		
2.	There is no competition between my partner and I in our relationship.		
3.	The partnership between my spouse and I is very strong and effective.		
4.	I never carry out a family or personal project without my partner knowing about it.		
5.	My partner never carries out a project without me knowing about it.		
6.	My life is incomplete without my partner's involvement in my life.		
7.	My actions and the actions of my partner complement each other.		
8.	My partner and I have committed to learn to work as a team.		
9.	My partner and I have agreed to cooperate to advance our mutual interests without disregarding our individual interests.		
10.	My partner and I are at liberty to contribute equally in the decision making process of our partnership, and we have high regard of each other's inputs.		

11.	My partner will always do what is best for me even if it is not best for him or her.		
12.	I will always do what is best for my partner even if it is not best for me. (selflessness in action)		
13.	In our true partnership as a couple, we treat each other equally and no one is regarded as inferior to the other, and the husband remains the head of the home.		
14.	My partner and I fully understand and agree what partnership means in our marriage relationship.		
15.	My partner and I fully understand and agree what authority and equality mean in our marriage relationship.		

Quiz Notes:
The quiz has 15 items, having an overall score of 150 means you are doing just fine in the *"element"* as far as the 15 items are concerned; and there is minimal enhancement or improvement that needs to be done. A score of 135 (90%) means tender loving attention is required on all items with a score of 5. A score of 120 (80%) and below means that quite a bit of work has to be done, because 20% or more of the items have scored 5 points each instead of 10. One may not comfortably say they have mastered or internalized Partnership in their relationship.

One has to do some serious introspection, and then further engage in a meaningful dialogue with the spouse about this. If things seem to be overwhelming, you still have the professional counselor on your side for guidance. Remember, the quiz is not the counselor, it only gives clues as to say, among others, what things you need to consider in your endeavor of improving Partnership in your relationship.

DOING THINGS TOGETHER

"Close relationship with your partner can help you to become the person you were meant to be through their encouragement and support."
(Drigotas, 2002).

As long as Adam and Eve were close together, the Devil's devious strategy could not work. He waited for a time when they were not together. You and your partner together form a powerful and formidable force that can conquer the challenging storms of marriage life, together you win. It is important to stay close to your spouse through the good times and bad times.

Just take a pause for a moment and ask yourself, *"What is it about your partner that made you want to spend a life's time with him or her?"* Doing things together does improve and increase bonding, relationship satisfaction, conflict resolution and communication amongst couples. When you struggle, struggle together and when you are happy having a good time, share the happiness together. Always be there for one another and you will definitely be happy with each other. The couple can also derive fulfilment and happiness from helping other people that are in need of what the couple can provide, even more so when they do it together.

The marriage relationship is very complicated and that is why the couple will not always have the perfect solutions to the challenges they face. They just need to learn how to navigate the challenging moments together in humility and respect to one another. There are a few ordinary things that partners can have fun when doing such together. These include the following among many;

- Taking a review of your marriage life together by talking about the good times or highlights of your marriage
- Reading a good book together
- Exercising, jogging or walking together
- Playing games together
- Taking a Bible study together
- Ministering to the needy together
- Taking a break or holiday together
- Doing work of charity together

Go through the challenges together other than blaming each other for not doing things differently during challenging times. Remember, there will always be the thought that one should have done things differently in the previous event or occasion. Every evening you should learn to reflect together on the good things that happened during each day of your lives. Partners should make it part of their lifestyle to share ideas and join hands to brainstorm and find solutions together. Marriage partners should also learn to put their synergy and creativity into finding ways of doing things better and differently where necessary. It is very much helpful to adopt a ***"team spirit"*** mentality as a couple, working together as a team makes the relationship to work better, especially when things reach a stage of getting more complicated, demanding, challenging and difficult.

High prevalence of counter-dependency characteristics could also pose a serious challenge to the flourishing of the relationship, especially in this element of togetherness. If the partners feel and think that they are well equipped, they may decide to deal with the counter-dependency challenge themselves. However, they may also get some help from a trusted source to assist them. It is always good to know what is challenging your marriage relationship and how to deal with it. For example, if you don't know the diagnosis of what makes you sick, then you won't have a clue as to what treatment to take, and you will remain sick if not sicker. ***Doing things together goes a long way in building that much needed trust in the relationship.***

Adam Gran says, *"Humble narcissists have very high expectations for their own success; but they also understand that great achievements are almost always the result of collective efforts."*

When you share good times together you are more likely to be next to each other, even in difficult times. That's the beauty of togetherness. Time together excludes time spent with children, friends and even relatives. ***By having time together, you are also building, emboldening and strengthening companionship.*** Let's get factual about this, making time for each other even when children and career demands are competing for the couple's best attention is of utmost importance. These challenges of life will not stop but the couple should be skillful and assertive enough as to how they use their limited time, also for the benefit of their marriage relationship.

The team spirit in the relationship could be improved by having trust in yourself, trusting your partner and standing by each other when challenges come up. When you do your part, be the best that you can be and always recognize and give respect to the efforts and ideas of your partner. Use your wisdom by accepting the constructive criticism from your partner without being defensive, even if you rightfully feel that you have to.

Teamwork gives space to one spouse to help the other, the more that space is allowed the stronger the bonding will become. This kind of situation makes it easy for the partners to have mutual agreements when necessary. It also makes the partners to become flexible to one another and to reach compromises easier than before. Bear in mind, any healthy relationship involves compromises now and again.

Doing things together has a positive impact on the couple's relationship, such that they become more closely connected and come to enjoy one another's company. Sharing the experiences together affords them to recognize something in common, which makes them feel good about each other. Some behavioral scientists are proponents of the 70/30 rule, which suggests that for the happiest, balanced and pleasant relationship; the couple should spend 70% of their time together and 30% being spent apart.

Well, as a proponent of togetherness myself, I'm not violently opposed to the suggestion; because, the 30% apart will afford the couples some needed space to fix a relationship that's breaking down and falling apart due to loss of individuality. The reality is that every healthy marriage relationship needs to make that individual space from time to time. The 30% time apart can make your relationship a whole lot stronger, when utilized accordingly and meaningfully. That moment of solitude for each partner is crucial and priceless. That's the time of reflection, refueling, recollection and rejuvenation for one's own self.

Some psychologists also suggest that partners should remember to tell each other how much they value one another by saying the two big words, ***"Thank You"*** and naming their specific efforts, and also letting them know how much they are appreciated by the other partner. Having mentioned all of this, I'm in support of the view that expressing gratitude and appreciation more often, goes a long way in keeping the relationship healthy and vibrant.

Working on the marriage relationship does not necessarily mean hard work. I suppose working smart on it makes the marriage relationship to be healthy and happy. Marriage relationship becomes hard work when we as couples, allow what does not belong to the marriage to come inside the marriage relationships; then such things will give us a "run-around" big time. That would mean hard work to restore peace back into the relationship, but I still say, "Together we win."

ANALOGY QUIZ: DOING THINGS TOGETHER			
No.	**ASSESSMENT STATEMENTS** (where 10 is most likely and 5 means it needs some tender loving attention)	**10**	**5**
1.	My partner and I work together smartly to make our marriage relationship healthy and happy.		
2.	Working on our marriage relationship does not always mean hard work.		
3.	We are skillful in allocating quality time for the two of us, our children, relatives, friends and for our career life.		
4.	Both in good times and bad times we are always together with my partner.		
5.	I found my partner to be a very supportive person in my life in all aspects.		
6.	I am a very supportive person in my partner's life in all aspects.		
7.	Doing things together has increased our bonding, relationship satisfaction, conflict resolution and communication in the marriage relationship.		
8.	We go through and navigate the challenges together other than blaming each other for the challenges in the relationship.		
9.	My partner and I have adopted a team spirit mentality so that we can come up with workable solutions together, especially when things are getting difficult and more challenging in the relationship.		

10.	My partner and I are the best friends ever, there's no space for anything else between us.		
11.	Doing things together motivates me, increases my potential and makes me to derive fulfilment and happiness in what I do with my partner.		
12.	Doing things together has made it easy to reach agreements and forge workable compromises in our marriage relationship.		
13.	Doing things together has improved our intimacy in all respects.		
14.	Doing things together has made us to open up and not be secretive to one another.		
15.	Over a period of time the quality of Doing things together has improved and strengthened the aspect of companionship in our relationship.		

Quiz Notes:
The quiz has 15 items, having an overall score of 150 means you are doing just fine in your good attempt to deal with the *"element"* as far as the 15 items are concerned. A score of 140 (93%) means tender loving attention is required on all items with a score of 5. A score of 120 (80%) and below means that quite a bit of work has to be done, because 20% or more of the items have scored 5 points each instead of 10. One may not comfortably say they have internalized some art and skill of dealing with Doing Things Together in their relationship.

One has to do some serious introspection, and then further engage in a meaningful dialogue with the spouse about this. If things seem to be overwhelming, you still have the professional counselor on your side for guidance. Remember, the quiz is not the counselor, it only gives clues as to say, among others, what things you need to consider in your endeavor of dealing with Doing Things Together in the relationship.

CHAPTER 7

TOLERANCE, HONESTY & PATIENCE

TOLERANCE

Let's look at the definitions of tolerance. Tolerance is being patient, understanding and accepting difference of opinions between you and your partner. It also displays the ability and willingness to tolerate the existence of opinions or behavior that one dislikes or disagrees with. According to some researchers, tolerance means capacity to endure pain or hardship. It may also mean endurance, fortitude, stamina, sympathy or indulgence for beliefs or practices differing from or conflicting with those of your own. In a nutshell, to be tolerant means that you accept your partner's opinions and preferences, even when they do not meet your own taste. Tolerance also means that you don't put your opinions above those of your partner, even when you are sure that you are right.

Have you ever heard somebody saying, ***"We do not love each other anymore in this marriage, and we are not happy but we are just tolerating each other."*** Well, that is a loaded statement and I 'm not talking about that kind of tolerance right now. Husband, at this moment, it is you and you only who is the husband to your wife. So, be the best husband that you can be to her. Wife, it is you at this moment, and you only who is the wife to your husband. So, be the best wife that you can be to him. I'm consciously saying this with polygamous marriages excluded. The human being has limited days under the sun, you cannot only learn from your own mistakes. So, do not be selfish, also learn from the mistakes that your partner makes.

Give each other some space to make those learning mistakes. Always remember that you are in this *"thing"* together. The legend Mahatma Ghandi said, *"We must be the change we wish to see in the world".* So, the change you want to see in your partner, must first begin with you tolerating your partner that you so much love. ***There is no "Mr Perfect Guy" or "Madam Perfect Lady". There is no perfect person, even no perfect couple for that matter.***

The synergy of marriage life has got more challenges than the life of singleness, because two totally different characters are merging to live together as one family. That is one of the reasons why there has to be a measure of tolerance in the marriage relationship. When you are in a bond of marriage, you need not to be selfish and self-centered by saying, *"It is my life."* ***Bear in mind now, it is no longer your life only and alone when you are married, because you are now living a shared life.*** Your spouse has a part and rule in your life and body and vice versa.

So, you need to embrace and tolerate that involvement of your partner in your life, you should not push your partner away; he or she is now part of your life and both of you need to connect. ***It is highly unlikely to talk about diversity and synergy without mentioning tolerance.*** The critical fact is that the marriage union is bringing different individuals that will never ever be the same, to come and live together to build a family. Marriage relationship should not be an intolerable situation where one partner is held hostage by the other intellectually, emotionally and otherwise.

HONESTY

In terms of definition, honesty is when you speak the truth and act truthfully. It is a combination of what comes out of your mouth from your heart and mind; and what you literally do by your actions. When you are honest to each other as a couple, it means that in word and in deed you are truthful and sincere to each other no matter what. You may rate yourself in the quiz below and later ask your partner to do the rating as well; when you compare the two ratings that will give you an idea as to what is your "thinking" about honesty in your marriage relationship. You may also get the opportunity to talk about how much you still need to do to work on this element of honesty.

My honest opinion is that happy marriages should reflect above average scores in most of the elements I'm discussing when it comes to the quizzes. Mark the phrase *"happy marriages"*, your marriage might not be perfect because there's no perfect marriage; but it can be a happy marriage.

Honesty is not openness but it links you to openness. A person may be honest but not open, a person can also be open but not honest. That is one reason why I am discussing these two elements separately. Every couple should not fail to understand that honesty has to do with the straightforwardness of talk and the straightforwardness of conduct. You walk the talk and your words should match your actions. Teach yourself to tell it like it is and no sugarcoating or word mincing. Every couple should take honesty as one of the foundational core values in their marriage relationship; when that is in place, no lie and deceit can defeat honesty.

Honesty brings about an emotion of fulfilment. It also shows the actuality and the authenticity of who you are.

Honesty hones and refines our thinking and perception, and allows us to be free of any thoughts of corruption of any kind. It empowers us to maintain uniformity and steadiness in the things we do, whilst at the same time gathering more credibility.

ANALOGY QUIZ: TOLERANCE & HONESTY			
No.	**ASSESSMENT STATEMENTS** (where 10 is most likely and 5 means it needs some tender loving attention)	**10**	**5**
1.	My partner gives me space to make mistakes and learn in our relationship.		
2.	I give my partner space to make mistakes and learn in our marriage relationship.		
3.	My partner understands me to be a very tolerant person.		
4.	I understand my partner to be a very tolerant person.		
5.	Tolerance goes along well with the diversity and synergy that are in our relationship.		
6.	I need to embrace and tolerate the involvement of my partner in my life.		
7.	We have accepted the fact that we are different individuals in the relationship and will never be the same, but we have to learn to live and work together.		
8.	As different as we are, we believe that we are the compatible and perfect couple to live together. Perfect in the sense that we are meant to be with each other.		
9.	On one to one conversation regarding any issue, my partner does not easily get tired of me.		

10.	On one to one conversation regarding any issue, I do not easily get tired of my partner.		
11.	I am able to tolerate the so called *"intolerables"* of my partner.		
12.	My partner is able to tolerate the so called *"intolerables"* of myself.		
13.	Tolerance is at its strongest point in our marriage relationship.		
14.	I talk straight to my partner without fear in our marriage relationship.		
15.	My partner talks straight to me without fear in our marriage relationship.		
16.	I have straightforwardness of talk and the straightforwardness of conduct.		
17.	My partner has straightforwardness of talk and the straightforwardness of conduct.		
18.	I am not just open, I am also honest in all my dealings in our marriage relationship.		
19.	My partner is not just open, I see her or him as being honest in all dealings in our marriage relationship.		
20.	In word and in deed I'm truthful and sincere to my partner no matter what.		
21.	In word and in deed my partner is truthful and sincere to me no matter what.		

22.	Honestly speaking, our marriage is not perfect but it is a good and happy marriage.		
23.	Because I'm honest, I'm also open to my partner.		
24.	Because my partner is honest, he or she is also open to me.		
25.	I walk the talk by matching my words with my actions.		
26.	My partner walks the talk by matching his/her words with actions.		

Quiz Notes:
The quiz has 26 items, having an overall score of 260 means you are doing just fine in the *"element"* as far as the 26 items are concerned; and there is minimal enhancement or improvement that needs to be done. A score of 235 (90%) means tender loving attention is required on all items with a score of 5. A score of 210 (80%) and below means that quite a bit of work has to be done, because 20% or more of the items have scored 5 points each instead of 10. One may not comfortably say they have internalized the concept of Tolerance & Honesty in their relationship.

One has to do some serious introspection, and then further engage in a meaningful dialogue with the spouse about this. If things seem to be overwhelming, you still have the professional counselor on your side for guidance. Remember, the quiz is not the counselor, it only gives clues as to say, among others, what things you need to consider in your endeavor of improving matters relating to Tolerance & Honesty in your relationship.

PATIENCE

Patience is defined as *"the capacity to accept or tolerate delay, trouble or suffering without getting angry, agitated or upset."* Patience is also a skill. We can work on increasing our ability to be patient and engage in practices to become more patient individuals.

Each partner in the marriage must be ready for surprises, especially from each other. Their ears, minds and hearts must be ready to hear things they thought they would never hear from each other. This is one of the most difficult matters in a marriage relationship ***to deal with in the wisdom and emotion it deserves.*** In a nutshell, ***the marriage is full of surprises that are both desirable and undesirable.*** When the desirable happens give thanks the Most-High God for His goodness and mercy, and you also do that by appreciating your spouse.

When the undesirable happens give thanks to the Almighty God that He has made you more than a conqueror even in this instance. In other words, show your spouse that you want to understand the situation and you want to do your positive best to handle it.

Regarding patience, it is better to listen to understand than listening to respond; because one may miss the point and cause more harm and argument than good. This element of patience is tested over and over again in a marriage relationship and not just once or twice, and partners must learn to be tenacious and resilient under all circumstances.

"Be completely humble and gentle; be patient, bearing with one another in love."
(Eph. 4:2).

In our way of life patience is essential and is also one of the key elements to our happiness. Having patience in one's possession means being able to wait calmly in the face of frustration, adversity, hostility, friction, enmity, bitterness or even resentment. We all have the opportunity to practice it.

What is distinctive and peculiar about the quality of being patient is its bearing of misfortune, provocation, annoyance, irritation or pain without complaint. It also illustrates an ability or willingness to suppress restlessness, loss of temper or annoyance when confronted with hindrance or delay.

There is a number of issues involved in patience. Patience may involve perseverance in the face of excessive waiting or retardation without irritation or getting bored. It provides tolerance of provocation without responding in disrespect or with anger. It shows forbearance when under strain, especially when faced with longer-term difficulties. Some of the psychological studies suggest that patience doesn't mean passivity or resignation, but power. It is also said to be an emotionally freeing practice of waiting, watching, and knowing when to act.

Some researchers suggest that the following may help us to develop some patience;

- Learning to be a patient listener
- Putting patience into practice
- Roll-back on unreasonable demands
- Embarking on long term view when making decisions
- Pursue ways to reduce stress levels
- Starting with yourself to be patient

- Make time out to be together with your partner bonding
- Learn and practice to accept the current reality in front of you
- Give your love time to grow
- Actively build a tolerance towards uncomfortable situations
- Accept the imperfection of your partner as well as that of yourself

One other key element to the quality of patience is redirecting of your attention to other important things. If you are solely focused on the thing you are awaiting to happen, the wait is likely to feel much more extended and perhaps, unbearable.

One psychological view hints that patience is a moral virtue because it contributes to happiness and living well. It further alludes that waiting attentively involves discerning when it's our turn to act; while waiting without complaint helps us not hate the waiting, but it helps us do our job well when it's our turn. This is very much applicable to our marriage relationships too. ***Just because you've battled with patience in the past doesn't mean you can't be more patient in the future.*** Patience is not a fixed quality, it's a skill that you can develop and improve. It is closely related to mercy and compassion.

Patience puts you in direct control of yourself, and there is no more powerful an aid to success than self-possession. When you are patient, you give yourself time to choose how to respond to a given situation, rather than to get emotionally overwhelmed by your emotions. It allows you as a couple to stay gathered no matter what is happening in your relationship. The power of patience calls on you as a couple to reclaim your time, your priorities, and your ability to respond to life with a firmly grounded sense of who you are. I concur with the view that it is the best gift next to love, which you soon learn that you can give to yourselves.

Instead of focusing on what is frustrating you in the short term, pay attention to resolving the main problem. Patience is not inherited but takes a whole lot of time and experience for it to be a part of our attributes. In some couples, it develops a bit quicker depending upon the intensity of their experience. Patience is a skill and not an inherited trait, feature or attribute I happened not to inherit. It leads to relaxation and it is not self-exploiting.

What does the Bible say about patience in marriage?

"Be completely humble and gentle; be patient, bearing with one another in love."
(Ephesians 4:8)

"Above all, love each other deeply, because love covers over a multitude of sins."
(1 Pet. 4:8)

The fourth fruit of the Spirit is patience.

ANALOGY QUIZ: PATIENCE			
No.	**ASSESSMENT STATEMENTS** (where 10 is most likely and 5 means it needs some tender loving attention)	**10**	**5**
1.	I understand that our marriage relationship will have both desirable and undesirable surprises.		
2.	When I am in disagreement with my partner, I always listen to understand than listening to respond.		
3.	I am aware and prepared that my patience will be tested more than once or twice in our marriage relationship.		
4.	In our marriage relationship, how do I rate my patience out of 10. (10 being the best).		
5.	In our marriage relationship, how would my partner rate my patience out of 10. (10 being the best).		
6.	I know my patience to be tenacious and resilient.		
7.	I know my partner's patience to be tenacious and resilient.		
8.	My self-possession through patience is very strong.		
9.	My partner's self-possession through patience is very strong.		
10.	I don't easily get hijacked by my emotions.		

11.	My partner does not easily get hijacked by his or her emotions.		
12.	I have already developed patience as a skill in my marriage relationship.		
13.	My partner has already developed patience as a skill in our marriage relationship.		

Quiz Notes:
The quiz has 13 items, and having an overall score of 130 means you doing just fine in this "element" as far as the 13 items are concerned; and there is minimal enhancement or improvement that needs to be done. Any score below 130-100 (83%) means tender loving attention is required on all items that score a 5. A score of 65 (50%) and below means that one has to do a lot of work to reach confidence level on this *"element"*. One has to do some serious introspection, and then further engage in a meaningful dialogue with the spouse. If things seem to be overwhelming, you still have the professional counselor on your side for guidance. Remember, the quiz is not the counselor, it only gives clues as to say, among others, what things you need to consider on your way to making your marriage happy as far as the element of Patience is concerned.

CHAPTER 8

RESPECT

Oxford languages dictionary defines respect as a feeling of deep admiration for others, as well as having due regard for feelings, wishes and rights of others. Respect is also defined as a characteristic of a "therapeutic" communication. The understanding is that when the communication between the partners is not a good one, it is highly unlikely to find respect being prevalent. Respect also means I treat my partner the way I want to be treated in return. Most partners like to react in a reciprocal way. In other words, they say, *"I did to him what he did to me. What's good for the goose is also good for the gander."* This sounds more of a revengeful type of thinking. It is not right to apply it to negative things, for example, where the first person has done a wrong thing to the second person.

Showing respect to someone is the evidence that they matter to you. When someone matters to you so much, you will definitely show some respect towards that person. I am of the view that respect is also affected by the role each spouse plays in the marriage relationship. For instance, if you are the husband the respect you show towards your wife is informed by the role you play as the husband and vice versa. The fact of the matter is that being disrespectful is being selfish to your partner; such as preferring to live one's life as one wishes, without considering the spouse's opinions and desires. This can breed disrespect towards one's partner.

It should be clearly understood that the two partners will never ever play exactly the same role in the marriage relationship. In simple terms, the husband is basically the provider to the wife, and the wife is basically the help-mate to the husband. So, husband be the best provider she's ever had, and wife be the best helpmate he's ever had and nothing worse to the contrary.

These are some of the pillars standing on the foundation of respect. Try not to become something contrary to what your role is ought to be in the marriage relationship, because the other spouse can easily and quickly pick that up; while the other spouse may easily and quickly switch to the denial mode when found on the wrong side. That kind of situation is not good for the relationship, deal with it as it plays out.

"7 In the same way, you husbands must give honour to your wives. Treat your wife with understanding as you live together. She may be weaker than you are, ***but she is your equal partner in God's gift of new life.*** *Treat her as you should so your prayers will not be hindered."*
(1 Peter 3:7 NLT).

Let's do a little bit of some introspection. Wife, are you the helpmate that he needs at his right hand in order to be the man he ought to be? Are you supporting him with all that you have? If not 100% sure, ask him what he thinks you need to be doing in order to be a good help-mate as far as he is concerned. Husband, are you the lover and provider she needs in her life in order to be the best helpmate you ever needed? Are you doing the best that you can to provide for her? If not 100% sure, ask her what she thinks you need to be doing in order to be the best lover and provider for her, as far as she is concerned.

This creates a good opportunity to give that dialogue a spark again. It may not be that easy but it is powerful and working. You may be surprised to find out that what you are busy doing, is not what your partner is expecting from you as far as demonstration of respect is concerned. So, talk about it.

Learn to give each other a chance to make good the errors of the past. Bear in mind, there is an element of reciprocity in respect, in other words, ***respect breeds respect and respect is earned and not just demanded from each other.*** When one partner is not doing what is expected of him or her in the relationship, it is easy to lose respect from the other partner. Stay put to playing your role as expected.

The human being is the most dynamic creation ever created on the face of the earth, and he has dominion over all other creatures on earth right down to the depth of the seas. Though he fell from God's grace but he hasn't lost his position in the heart of God.

"...4what is man that You are mindful of him, or the son of man that You care for him? 5You made him a little lower than the angels; You crowned him with glory and honor. 6You made him ruler of the works of Your hands; You have placed everything under his feet:..."
(Ps. 8:4-6 BSB).

The wife should respect the husband because, the husband is made to be very effective in the family relationship through the respect that is given to him by her. The husband should love the wife because, the wife is made to be very effective in the family relationship through the love that is given and demonstrated towards her by him.

Perhaps I can sum it up and say, ***"A loving husband makes a happy and respectful wife, and a respectful wife makes a happy and loving husband."***

Disrespect in the relationship compromises the love that the partners have for each other. The love spark may seem meaningless as a result of disrespect even though it is there in existence. Respect your spouse for his or her suggestions, opinions, talents, values, standards, principles, choices and capabilities. ***Admire the way he or she is different from you.*** When your partner talks, respect will always make you to listen actively and attentively to understand him or her without being negative and defensive, no matter what mood you are in.

Crossing your partner's boundaries such as values, standards and principles equals invasion of one's personal life. It is more like a take-over of your partner's personal life and dictating how he or she should live it. Showing respect to such boundaries will strengthen the relationship and sustain its happiness. ***Let every request to your partner be respectful and not demanding.*** Respect also shows value and appreciation to your partner.

"A gentle answer deflects anger, but harsh words make tempers flare."
(Prov. 15:1 NLT).

Bear in mind, each marriage relationship has got its own temper "flare-ups", the couples should be aware of its triggers and manage them.

ANALOGY QUIZ: RESPECT			
No.	ASSESSMENT STATEMENTS (where 10 is most likely and 5 means it needs some tender loving attention)	10	5
1.	My partner is having due regard to my feelings, wishes and my other rights.		
2.	I am having due regard to my partner's feelings, wishes and his or her other rights.		
3.	My partner always treats me the way he or she wants to be treated in return.		
4.	I always treat my partner the way I want to be treated in return.		
5.	My partner's demonstration of respect reflects what I expect from him or her.		
6.	I think my demonstration of respect reflects what my partner expects from me.		
7.	My partner gives me some chance to make good of my errors.		
8.	I give my partner a chance to make good of his or her errors.		
9.	The value of respect is very much prevalent in our relationship.		
10.	My partner never swears or throw insults at me.		
11.	I never swear or throw insults at my partner.		

12.	We have a workable way of dealing with disrespect whenever it tries to disturb our marriage relationship.		
13.	Disrespect is an unwanted behavior, so it should be addressed without fear.		
14.	There is no acceptable excuse for disrespect in our marriage relationship.		
15.	Respect breeds respect and respect is earned and not just demanded from each other in the relationship.		

Quiz Notes:
The quiz has 15 items, having an overall score of 150 means you are doing just fine in the *"element"* as far as the 15 items are concerned; and there is minimal enhancement or improvement that needs to be done. A score of 135 (90%) means tender loving attention is required on all items with a score of 5. A score of 120 (80%) and below means that quite a bit of work has to be done, because 20% or more of the items have scored 5 points each instead of 10. One may not comfortably say they have internalized the concept of Respect in their relationship.

One has to do some serious introspection, and then further engage in a meaningful dialogue with the spouse about this. If things seem to be overwhelming, you still have the professional counselor on your side for guidance. Remember, the quiz is not the counselor, it only gives clues as to say, among others, what things you need to consider in your endeavor of improving matters relating to Respect in your relationship.

CHAPTER 9

CONSIDERATION & OPENNESS

CONSIDERATION

Consideration in a marriage relationship means thoughtfulness for your partner. It may also relate to attention or a compassionate regard for your spouse. In a nutshell, consideration may be defined as kindness and thoughtful regard for others, or an act of thoughtfulness. This means treating others as you would have them treat you. When you give something consideration, you think about it carefully, and not too quickly.

Let your decisions be well-thought and not taken hastily, and your spouse will derive value in that, because your decisions will reflect some quality. Some definitions define consideration as a reason for doing something based on natural affection, generosity, love, or moral duty. It also involves thinking about other people's feelings and needs. ***Consideration reflects selflessness and not selfishness.***

Make space, time and effort to think about what your partner has invested in the relationship. This increases your appreciation and positive feelings towards your spouse and elevates the marriage commitment to another level. That is another way of triggering happiness and you will remain grateful. Consideration also means doing things for your partner which you would necessarily not do for own purposes, and you do them for the sake of making your spouse happy; and that actually involves sacrifice. Say thank you even for the little things, and voice out your appreciation always. Each partner should show some consideration and focus on things that would make the marriage relationship better for both of them.

You have to work on your marriage relationship yourself. God will not do it for you, but He will help you do it if you want to. So, do not be lazy and blame God when things do not look good in the relationship, go ahead and do what is expected of you. Actually, it is your own marriage and it is not God who is married to your spouse, but you.

Marriage is a choice in life and not a requirement for you to live. After all, the reality is that you can live and make it in life without it, so, it is your choice in life.

So, consideration in the relationship means being considerate and honoring the feelings, opinions and belongings of your partner. It also involves making responsible choices and actions not to disregard the individualism of the other partner with its rights, preferences and privileges. This may include in some instances the putting aside of your own self so that the other partner is not hurt.

What I also mean is that, I must be mindful of the fact that I should not only be focusing at achieving my personal goals at the expense of my partner's peace and happiness in the relationship. The analogy quiz statements may also help the couple to have conversation on a number of things concerning consideration. The couple may end up getting alignment on things where there was no alignment before, even on matters they thought not to be easy to start a dialogue about. Your life will never be the same after engaging in a meaningful dialogue session with your partner concerning consideration.

OPENNESS

Openness is defined as lack of secrecy or concealment. It may also be classified as a personality trait. Being open to one another as a couple in all matters of the marriage relationship builds up trust to a stronger level. If there are issues that you cannot talk about with your partner, then you might not be open as you should. Your partner should feel, hear and understand your heartbeat so to speak. Your partner cannot see what is inside your heart and mind, he or she can only get in there through your openness. Spouses should not hide serious matters that affect their marriage relationship from each other.

There are things that a spouse may think, that the other spouse would have been a better person if he or she had them, but the other spouse will not know until told about such things. Let me put it this way; I should be open enough to my wife by asking her, what things according to her way of thinking would make me a better husband if I had them. If she is open enough about our relationship she should speak her heart and mind out. I should be able to do the same to her. If you have been together for a while as a couple, your spouse almost knows you better than yourself in some areas; and should be in a better position to give some advice as to what to do to improve, and this time you should listen very carefully to that ***"expert"*** advice.

Here is a simple example, if my wife says that I would be a better husband if I had patience; then as far as she knows me, she should give me some suggestions as to what I should do to build that patience in me. She may even tell me some hindrances she sees that may be blocking the patience to manifest out of my character. Some hindrances and shortcomings I may not be seeing them by myself, but she might have been seeing them all the time but the atmosphere in the relationship was not conducive to openness. ***When you make a break through to this openness element make good use of it, it may transform your relationship big time.***

The crux of the matter is that, do not allow the openness to be the beginning of fighting with each other, that's childish. Don't miss out, this is the grand opportunity to take-off some unnecessary heavy loads from your marriage relationship and allow it to transform itself to happiness. ***Openness takes away heaviness and gives you freedom.*** Partners should not be loud when they deal with issues that come out of openness, they should learn to deal with these issues calmly and peaceably. Opening up to justify yourself will defeat the purpose, of course self- justification is not what you want to achieve. Both of you want to improve your marriage relationship to the better.

You should be an open book to one another such that if any partner wants to do some tests in the relationship, it would be an open book test. However, if the relationship is full of hidden secrets and concealment where some things are prevented from being known to each other, that becomes a recipe for disaster. Therefore, consideration and openness when internalized and practiced by the couples, could lead to good and happy marriages.

ANALOGY QUIZ: CONSIDERATION & OPENNESS			
No.	**ASSESSMENT STATEMENTS** (where 10 is most likely and 5 means it needs some tender loving attention)	**10**	**5**
1.	My partner knows me to be a very considerate person.		
2.	I know my partner to be a very considerate person.		
3.	I fully understand what it means to be considerate in the relationship.		
4.	I think my partner fully understands what it means to be considerate in the relationship.		
5.	I am fully aware of what my partner has invested in our relationship.		
6.	My partner is fully aware of what I have invested in our relationship.		
7.	I have shown appreciation of my partner's efforts and sacrifices in building and strengthening our relationship.		
8.	My partner has shown appreciation of my efforts and sacrifices in building and strengthening our relationship.		
9.	Individualism of each partner with its rights, preferences and privileges is highly respected in our relationship.		
10.	I value what my partner has invested in our marriage relationship.		

11.	My partner values what I have invested in our marriage relationship.		
12.	I can see selflessness and not selfishness in my partner.		
13.	My partner can see selflessness and not selfishness in me.		
14.	Thoughtfulness is one value that is very much prevalent in our relationship.		
15.	We are always willing to do that extra mile to keep happiness in our relationship.		
16.	There's no secrecy or concealment of matters between us in our relationship.		
17.	Opening up to each other in all matters of our marriage relationship builds up trust to a stronger level.		
18.	My partner cannot see my heart and mind until I open up to him or her about them.		
19.	We should be open enough about our relationship and each partner should speak his or her heart and mind out.		
20.	We feel each other's heartbeat and understand each other's mind as a couple.		

Quiz Notes:

The quiz has 20 items, having an overall score of 200 means you are doing just fine in the *"element"* as far as the 20 items are concerned; and there is minimal enhancement or improvement that needs to be done. A score of 180 (90%) means tender loving attention is required on all items with a score of 5. A score of 160 (80%) and below means that quite a bit of work has to be done, because 20% or more of the items have scored 5 points each instead of 10. One may not comfortably say they have internalized Consideration & Openness in their relationship.

One has to do some serious introspection, and then further engage in a meaningful dialogue with the spouse about this. If things seem to be overwhelming, you still have the professional counselor on your side for guidance. Remember, the quiz is not the counselor, it only gives clues as to say, among others, what things you need to consider in your endeavor of improving Consideration & Openness in the relationship.

CHAPTER 10

SHARING AND GENEROSITY

SHARING

As an individual and a partner in a marriage relationship, you should be at peace with the fact that not everything you have is for you alone. Now the language has since changed completely, it is no longer my money, my income, my cash bonus, my house, my car, my ministry, my family and so forth. The word *"my"* has been substituted with *"our"* because another person has entered into your life to share it with you. It is not good practice to allow materialism to come in between the two of you. As a couple you should be enjoying everything jointly with one another.

Sharing compels the partners to learn more about the importance of fair-mindedness and compromise in the relationship. The sharing gesture means you value the person you are sharing something with, otherwise you could have been uncaring and selfish. This includes sharing your quality time, love, the outdoors, space and other resources. Sharing is caring, when spouses share they show that they care for one another dearly. ***When sharing willingly with the other partner, means that you value the partner more than the things you are sharing; bear in mind that these things are not who you are but they are what you have.*** So sharing them will make you and your partner happy.

What is also factual is that if you want to stay connected to your partner, you need to be in a sharing mode in all aspects of the relationship including feelings in addition to the materialistic things.

GENEROSITY

The Oxford Languages dictionary defines generosity as the quality of being kind and generous. Whereas, the Merriam-Webster dictionary says that generosity is the quality of being kind, understanding, and not selfish. Generosity is also defined as bigheartedness, liberality, openhandedness and openheartedness. It is also associated with kindness and being considerate of the other person. This is all facilitated by willingness, because a willing heart can achieve great things. In the perspective of the Holy Writ, generosity can be seen as the act of being a ***"Good Samaritan"*** to the other person, off course, with your spouse included. Playing "Good Samaritan" to each other nourishes and nurtures the marriage relationship, because that chases away the hostilities between the partners; and rather makes them to be even more considerate to one another.

The fact of the matter is that generosity should be seen as an act of freewill without any obligation. Remember, you apply your freedom of choice and choose to be generous, that is why a generous person will always be happy when doing it. The way I see it is that you freely and willfully give something of your own that is of value to the other person without obligation. What is nice and beautiful in this is that, you are consciously aware that you are exercising your own freedom to do something good for the other person. In other words, ***you still feel that the power is yours and you are not being victimized but you are being generous by choice.*** One may also be generous by being supportive or providing any kind of help.

Each spouse must be willing to let go and give away certain rights and privileges to the other in a marriage relationship. This should be done with the aim of giving chance for peace and happiness to prevail. It is natural to keep and protect your own and un-intentionally switching to a selfish mode, then you get phrases like; *"my money, my efforts, my sacrifices, my things, and so forth".* It is a fact that what is mine is mine and what is yours is yours, but what is important is combining the two sides to function as one unit. Being generous as person also reflects the selflessness that is enshrined in the person's character so to speak. I mean caring so much for the well-being of others, specifically your spouse.

The Holy Writ also says that the two shall be one. It does not say that the one shall be one because it recognizes that a couple is made up of two different individuals, who should synergistically function as one unit. If that is not the case, where does generosity and sharing really fit in among couples. Generosity is also one characteristic of philanthropy, where the *"haves"* are mindful of the happiness of the *"have not's".*

Even in a marriage relationship, the strengths and capabilities of partners are not the same, so don't be too possessive by saying; my money, my idea, my plan, my contribution, my effort, my car, my house, my children, my clothes, my food and so forth. It is better to say; our money, our idea, our contribution, our plan, our effort, our house, our children, our car, you name it.

This sounds very much calming, soothing and encouraging in a relationship. Just listen to this, *"Why should I be generous to you when you once did this selfish and bad thing to me?"* Generosity is ungrudging, it does not ask such a question but it always does good to others all the time. Generosity is giving without necessarily expecting the same in return. Generosity does not count how much I am spending on my partner to keep him or her happy. Being generous also reflects the principle and moral practice of concern for happiness of other people which is called **altruism**. It is said that altruism results in a quality of life both materially and spiritually. Generosity works hand in hand with compassionate love.

ANALOGY QUIZ: SHARING & GENEROSITY			
No.	ASSESSMENT STATEMENTS (where 10 is most likely and 5 means it needs some tender loving attention)	10	5
1.	Materialism is not the master in our relationship, but we master materialism.		
2.	My partner is the one who likes to share in the relationship.		
3.	I am the one who likes to share in the relationship.		
4.	We both equally like to share in the relationship.		
5.	I am fair and offer some compromises in the relationship.		
6.	My partner is fair and offer some compromises in the relationship.		
7.	I value my partner more than the things I share with him or her.		
8.	My partner values me more than the things he or she shares with me.		
9.	I am not a selfish person in our relationship.		
10.	My partner is not a selfish person in our relationship.		
11.	Sharing has helped us to stay connected in the relationship.		

12.	My partner knows me to be a generous and ungrudging person in our relationship.		
13.	I know my partner to be a generous and ungrudging person in our relationship.		
14.	My partner is always willing to compromise for the sake of peace and happiness in our relationship.		
15.	I am always willing to compromise for the sake of peace and happiness in our relationship.		
16.	I fully agree that what I have is not just mine but ours in the relationship.		
17.	My partner fully agrees that what he or she has is ours in the relationship.		
18.	I am always willing to go an extra mile in order to make my partner happy.		
19.	My partner is always willing to go an extra mile in order to make me happy.		
20.	I easily share time, gifts, eatables and money with my partner.		
21.	My partner easily shares time, gifts, eatables and money with me.		
22.	My partner does not count how much money is spent on me to make me happy.		
23.	I do not count how much money is spent on my partner to make him or her happy.		

24.	I exercise my freedom of choice very well and I am generous by choice.		
25.	My partner does not demand my generosity, it happens spontaneously from me.		
26.	I do not demand generosity from my partner, it happens spontaneously from him or her.		

Quiz Notes:
The quiz has 26 items, having an overall score of 260 means you are doing just fine in the *"element"* as far as the 26 items are concerned; and there is minimal enhancement or improvement that needs to be done. A score of 235 (90%) means tender loving attention is required on all items with a score of 5. A score of 210 (80%) and below means that quite a bit of work has to be done, because 20% or more of the items have scored 5 points each instead of 10. One may not comfortably say they have internalized the concept of Sharing & Generosity in their relationship.

One has to do some serious introspection, and then further engage in a meaningful dialogue with the spouse about this. If things seem to be overwhelming, you still have the professional counselor on your side for guidance. Remember, the quiz is not the counselor, it only gives clues as to say, among others, what things you need to consider in your endeavor of improving matters relating to Sharing & Generosity in your relationship.

CHAPTER 11

MONEY MATTERS

Couples need to take time and talk about their finances in their marriage, this should be a regular activity in their relationship. In a way of handling your finances, you should craft a strategy that will work well for both of you. Practically, you may like to discuss how you will merge your finances such that there is no tension between the two of you. It is also better for partners to know each other's credit scores. That would assist in paving the way towards financial peace in the relationship, because the likelihood is that each partner would talk about improving their credit scores if that is necessary. If you like staying debt free, well for now, the credit score wouldn't be something to worry about.

The married couples also need to understand the impact of inflation and the time value of money in the finances of their marriage relationship. Partners need to learn to budget together such that, it would not be one partner who is doing it alone and finalize matters without the consent of the other. When one partner does it without consent of the other, he or she may lose the correct objectivity as far as the partnership of the marriage relationship is concerned. That may cause the unnecessary and undesirable friction concerning money matters.

Concerning the inflation and the time value of money, it has been discovered by economists that a R100 will be worth R50 in ten years' time. In other words, the value of money drops by 50% every ten years based on the South African economic perspective. Whether you keep it in the bank or under the matrass, this philosophy applies. In a nutshell, the buying power of 1 rand or 1 dollar decreases every year.

The common philosophy of ***"Spend now and save later"*** does not help the relationship very well. However, the one which says, ***"Save now and spend later"*** does assist the relationship big time in the near future concerning money matters. Please bear in mind, the money that you correctly save and invest will always be there for you and you will never miss it; but the one that is spent will always be gone forever. The above simple philosophy highlights the importance of understanding the issue of savings and investment when it comes to money matters. It is also beneficial to understand income generation, expenditure categories, assets and liabilities. Another very crucial aspect is that of understanding debt or credit and how does it fit into the marriage relationship finances.

It sounds and feels good to surprise each other with gifts and good things in the marriage relationship, however, the happiness coming with the surprise might be short-lived if the surprise was as a result of undiscussed debt. The debt comes with medium to long-term financial constraints that may cause serious challenges to the relationship. In order to be happy in the relationship you have to wisely decide together to get into debt, and not one partner without the knowledge and agreement of the other. Getting into debt should be a calculated risk done mutually by both spouses.

It is also not healthy in the relationship for one partner to tell the other and say, *"I just bought a new car or expensive furniture on a hire purchase agreement payable in six years."* This means that the financial cash flow of the married couple will be negatively affected for the next six years; and that has not been mutually discussed and agreed upon by both partners. It is highly beneficial when the couple make use of the services of a financial advisor when necessary, regarding financial matters.

Whether by agreement or by one partner's decision, both of you may eventually get into debt; but the difference between the two is that you will get into debt wisely and with peace of mind when you do it together. It is very crucial for the partners to understand each other's attitude towards debt. ***It is common for a couple to have different if not opposing views on money matters.***

In your endeavor of working your relationship towards a happy and successful one; educate yourselves on money matters and learn to handle them together regardless of your differences. That will work out wonders in the relationship as far as money is concerned. The *"Money Matters Concept"* with its challenges is rated by some researchers as the number one cause of divorce in the USA. In South Africa, it is rated number two cause of divorce in the country, where number one is lack of good communication. So, as married couples we need to make sure that this part of our lives is in good hands and under control.

Let me quickly touch the issue of budgeting concerning the area where disagreements tend to arise. Let each spouse draft the family budget for the month. Each one should then explain his or her budget to the other. The couple should discuss and align the differences and then compile together a new monthly budget for the family. There should be clear sources of income showing how the agreed upon family budget would be financed. Try to reach consensus and implement the budget. The couple should also agree on the standard of living acceptable to both of them, which should off course be in alignment with their affordable budget.

ANALOGY QUIZ: MONEY MATTERS			
No.	**ASSESSMENT STATEMENTS** (where 10 is most likely and 5 means it needs some tender loving attention)	**10**	**5**
1.	I take money matters seriously in our marriage relationship.		
2.	My partner takes money matters seriously in our marriage relationship.		
3.	The state of our money matters is healthy in the relationship.		
4.	We make time to talk about our finances frequently as a couple.		
5.	Money matters now do not cause tension in our relationship.		
6.	We have an up-to-date will for each of us as a couple.		
7.	I know my partner's credit score and he or she knows mine.		
8.	I do not buy on credit and make cash loans without my partner knowing about it.		
9.	My partner does not buy on credit and make cash loans without me knowing about it.		
10.	I am good and not bad when it comes to monthly spending.		
11.	My partner is very disciplined when it comes to monthly spending.		

12.	I can confidently say that our money matters are in good hands.		
13.	We are doing a good job concerning our monthly budget, it's still working well for us.		
14.	We have our own financial advisor as a couple, for other financial matters.		
15.	If we run into trouble with our finances, we are able to bounce back and self-correct.		

Quiz Notes:

The quiz has 15 items, having an overall score of 150 means you are doing just fine in the *"element"* as far as the 15 items are concerned; and there is minimal enhancement or improvement that needs to be done. A score of 135 (90%) means tender loving attention is required on all items with a score of 5. A score of 120 (80%) and below means that quite a bit of work has to be done, because 20% or more of the items have scored 5 points each instead of 10. One may not comfortably say they have internalized the concept of Money Matters in their relationship. One has to do some serious introspection, and then further engage in a meaningful dialogue with the spouse about this. If things seem to be overwhelming, you still have the professional counselor on your side for guidance. Remember, the quiz is not the counselor, it only gives clues as to say, among others, what things you need to consider in your endeavor of improving matters relating to Money Matters in your relationship.

CHAPTER 12

WILLINGNESS TO COMPROMISE

Compromise is defined as an agreement over a dispute reached by each side, changing or giving up some demands after much argument. It is commonly understood as giving up something, in order to reach a place of understanding with your partner. No two partners are the same. Somewhere in the relationship you and your partner will have a different viewpoint, perspective or proposal.

Another definition would be that compromise is when two sides give up some demands to meet each other in the halfway, this also means settlement of a dispute by concessions on both sides of the relationship. It is also a concept of securing an agreement through finding a middle ground. I would also say, it is when the partners come to terms with one another by settling a dispute by mutual concession. This means that the original plans, ambitions, goals, objectives might have to be changed or altered a little bit by one or both parties.

It is natural that in times of distress you go through from one side to the other side and still be holding your own, even when all odds are pointing to the contrary. I mean when it is not even necessary but pointless. It's also human to always want to win an argument, as human beings we always like to compete with one another such as ***"keeping up with the Joneses or Khumalo's"*** next door. Spouses may often times find themselves competing with one another in the marriage relationship over a number of things.

There might also be an element of wanting to out-smart each other, and that may cause some kind of unwanted friction between the couple. It takes the willingness and the ability of each partner, to bring a compromise that will harmoniously end every argument that disturbs happiness in the relationship. Compromise is not an easy element to adopt and put to practice, but willfully it can be learned, aligned and then standardized into the relationship. There will be issues about each other's behavior and habits that you will not be impressed with. Over a period of time they become glaring and a little bit annoying if one takes notice at them long enough, ***bear in mind, every rose has its own set of thorns.***

If the things that you seem not to like about your partner are not life-threatening to both of you, you may as well be at peace and start to embrace that difference. That way you will subtly learn to live with it peacefully and enjoyably. Frankly speaking, you need to appreciate and enjoy each other's differences and that is the better compromise, not only for the two of you but also for your relationship. ***The best compromise for a married couple is that of forgiveness between each other on a permanent basis.***

Have you ever heard somebody talking to you or to somebody else saying something like this, *"I'm so glad that you are not like me, you are so generous and very much accommodating even when I've been uneasy to you; and I'm saying this amid your not so good budgeting habits; but at least our kids have their school fees paid for, have school shoes, church shoes and running shoes."*

When you have trained your mind to be flexible, you should find it easy to change habits, including those that do more harm than good in the marriage relationship. By doing this you are taking care of yourself whilst also taking care of your spouse and the relationship. So, everyone benefits from your mental flexibility.

As unique individuals, we are having a number of different stereotypes about different things and different people in life. You will have your own stereotypes on finances, childrearing, education and so forth. So, it is better to talk about each other's stereotypes and understand them, before even talking about possible disputations concerning some of the stereotypes. My view is that a partner should not dispute the other partner's stereotype until it is thoroughly understood, and found to be threatening or negatively affecting the marriage relationship.

Other than that, the partners should learn to live with each other's stereotypes peacefully without wasting time on disputations. Remember, each of you is uniquely unique and your stereotypes about things and people may not be the same

ANALOGY QUIZ: WILLINGNESS TO COMPROMISE			
No.	**ASSESSMENT STATEMENTS** (more Yes's than No's means some tender loving attention is needed)	**YES**	**NO**
1.	When I get into argument or confrontation with my partner, at the end I would still be holding my own view always, no matter how right or wrong.		
2.	When my partner gets into argument or confrontation with me, at the end he or she would still be holding his or her view always, no matter how right or wrong.		
3.	My partner does not understand what compromise means in our relationship.		
4.	I do not understand what compromise means in our relationship.		
5.	I always want to win the argument in our relationship.		
6.	My partner always wants to win the argument in our relationship.		
7.	When having an argument with me, often times my partner does not want to make a compromise in order to end it in harmony.		
8.	When having an argument with my partner, often times I do not want to make a compromise in order to end it in harmony.		

9.	For me to compromise means I have become a weakling and useless victim.		
10.	For my partner to compromise he or she thinks of having become a weakling and useless victim.		
11.	I think compromise is not a wise strategic move to take our relationship forward.		
12.	My partner sees compromise as not a wise strategic move to take our relationship forward.		

Quiz Notes:

The quiz has 12 negative statements with the option of classifying each statement with a "yes" if you agree with it, and with a "no" when you disagree with it. If you score 8 statements with a "yes", that will mean your intelligence is not friendly to the concept of Willingness to Compromise in your marriage relationship; and this may be in one way or the other not beneficial to you. A score of 6 statements with a "yes" and below to 3 would mean that, your intelligence might still be a bit hostile towards Willingness to Compromise. One has to do some serious introspection, and then further engage in a meaningful dialogue with the spouse. Perhaps one would express valid reasons for the "yes" and "no" responses at his or her own right. I suppose that the couple would also learn how to strike a balance on issues like these in the process. If things seem to be overwhelming, you still have the professional counselor on your side for guidance. Remember, the quiz is not the counselor, it only gives clues as to say, among others, what things you need to consider on your way to making the Willingness to Compromise useful and meaningful to your marriage relationship.

CHAPTER 13

EMBRACING CONSTRUCTIVE CRITICISM

Constructive criticism is defined as a helpful way of giving someone feedback that provides specific, actionable or workable suggestions. Other than providing general advice, constructive criticism gives specific recommendations on how to make positive improvements. It is clear to the point and easy to put into action.

The focus of constructive criticism is to provide constructive feedback which is backed up by specific examples, in order to help one to improve in a specific area. However, this should be given in a friendly manner and with good intentions. When the criticism is truly constructive, it will be well-intentioned such that the behavior of the person given to, or his/her work will somehow improve. If the criticism does not offer clear guidelines on how one can improve behavior, perhaps it may not be truly constructive.

When you are receiving constructive criticism from your partner, you are gaining a new perspective on how you can improve, which can give you another opportunity to observe things you missed before; and encourage you to try a different approach to what you normally do. In a marriage relationship set-up, constructive criticism is in contrast to more confrontational forms of criticism in which a partner is unkind or threatening when offering feedback. The intent of aggressive criticism is to hurt someone's feelings, whereas ***constructive criticism serves as a form of feedback that is intended to improve a relationship.***

Let's talk about how to make this thing work. Learn to criticize the wrong action and not the person. In other words, you should address the bad behavior and not the personality of the person. You also do this by starting on a positive note and ending on a positive note during a conversation with your partner. The idea is that each partner should always learn to habitually give positive feedback to the other partner. Don't talk about last week's mistakes again and again.

The change you want to see in your marriage relationship should first begin with you, that's the correct mindset to start with. If you point out a problem in the relationship, try to bring a suggested solution also, that will show the very constructive side of you. Trying to be defensive when receiving feedback doesn't help at all. In the process, each partner should try to understand each other's reasoning.

You may even wish to show your partner the wrong habit that you have improved on, that will create good ground for you to be taken seriously going forward. When you have nothing to show in terms of improvement, it will be difficult to point out faults in the relationship as far as your other partner is concerned. Bear in mind, our marriage relationships are marked by a combination of friendship and conflict.

Gently correct your partner when he or she is wrong. What is discouraging is when the wrong partner arrogantly rejects a gentle and friendly correction. ***Don't sound like an ingrate when somebody who loves you corrects you when you***

are wrong. Remember that both of you are human beings that are perfectly imperfect. As partners you need to work on things that build each other's self-esteem, and indirectly you will be boosting each other's self-worth in the marriage relationship. One should take cognizance of the fact that arrogance is also caused by insecurity as a result of low self-esteem. Do not forget the fact that each partner has his or her own subjective opinions about life, that is why you find yourselves doing things differently to each other. However, the healthy dialogue will help you to always find each other when you happen to miss one another along the way. It helps to know why do I think the way I think as a person, so that I can self-correct when I realize that I'm going in the wrong direction. Constructive criticism may come handy to conscientize a person in this regard.

Learn to love yourself unconditionally and unapologetically, and then you will be able to learn to also allow the other spouse to be who they are. Bear in mind, it took years and a lot of support from each other to be where you are today as a couple. ***So, remain bold and courageous in supporting each other no matter the circumstances.***

"I can do all things through Christ who strengthens me." (Phil. 4:13 NKJV).

This verse helps you to develop your self-esteem and self-trust. Don't run away but always show up for your partner especially in times of need. Constructive criticism doesn't only tell a person the wrongs but also tells what should be done to make things right. Dialogue is not a fight, once it starts as a fight of words it is no longer a dialogue but an argument. That is not good enough for the relationship; to be constructive in your criticism, you need to learn even from the mistakes of life that you and others make with your spouse included.

In life, it is not always because you started wrong and that you will end-up wrong because you should have started the right way; no, that is a wrong formula as far as I am concerned. The Apostle Paul started his gospel ministry as a murderer but God turned things around in his life. God the Almighty can turn things around in your marriage too, never ever lose hope even for one minute. ***He specializes on things thought impossible by some couples.*** He does things that no man or other power can do.

The tool of constructive criticism should be viewed as a convenient and practical feedback that can help you improve yourself rather than putting you down. Another reality is that, when criticism is constructive it is usually easier to accept, even though it still hurts a little bit; perhaps for my good.

ANALOGY QUIZ: EMBRACING CONSTRUCTIVE CRITICISM			
No.	**ASSESSMENT STATEMENTS** (where 10 is most likely and 5 means it needs some tender loving attention)	**10**	**5**
1.	I fully understand what constructive criticism means in our marriage relationship.		
2.	My partner fully understands what constructive criticism means in our relationship.		
3.	When I criticize I aim to correct the error and build our relationship to be better.		
4.	I always accept my partner's constructive criticism towards me.		
5.	My partner always accepts my constructive criticism towards him or her.		
6.	I do believe in constructive criticism and I focus on dealing with the problem and not the person's personality.		
7.	My partner corrects me gently and friendly when I am wrong.		
8.	I correct my partner gently and friendly when he or she is wrong.		
9.	Constructive criticism is very much helpful to our marriage relationship.		
10.	I find it easy and practical to make use of constructive criticism in our relationship.		

11.	I fully agree with the fact that constructive criticism is a convenient and practical feedback that can help me to improve myself rather than putting me down.		
12.	Even though constructive criticism may hurt a little bit, I'm still willing to accept it from my partner.		
13.	Providing constructive feedback to one another does not end up in a confrontational session between us as a couple.		
14.	The change I want to see in my marriage relationship should first begin with me.		
15.	Yes, I know I can do it because, *"I can do all things through Christ who strengthens me."*		

Quiz Notes:
The quiz has 15 items, having an overall score of 150 means you are doing just fine in the *"element"* as far as the 15 items are concerned; and there is minimal enhancement or improvement that needs to be done. A score of 135 (90%) means tender loving attention is required on all items with a score of 5. A score of 120 (80%) and below means that quite a bit of work has to be done, because 20% or more of the items have scored 5 points each instead of 10. One may not comfortably say they have internalized the issue of Embracing Constructive Criticism in their relationship.

One has to do some serious introspection, and then further engage in a meaningful dialogue with the spouse about this. If things seem to be overwhelming, you still have the professional counselor on your side for guidance. Remember, the quiz is not the counselor, it only gives clues as to say, among others, what things you need to consider in your endeavor of improving matters relating to Embracing Constructive Criticism in your relationship.

CHAPTER 14

GOOD MANAGEMENT OF ARGUMENTS

I concur and subscribe to the fact that no marriage relationships are the same, they are all different in their own rights and respects. Besides, the problems and challenges that face them all do not care about that, they just attack them all irrespective of their uniqueness in the relationship equation. Just like the pandemic attacking the rich and the poor, the safe and the unsafe alike. So, it is important for each couple to make analysis of their own relationship, and learn to understand the possible challenges that are likely to be more frequent than others in their unique relationship.

Then, your mitigation strategy is likely to be stronger and effective in dealing with the challenges you face as a couple. ***Please understand this from the start, it is all about doing something about your relationship as a couple. You cannot just sit and expect every good thing to come automatically on a platter to you.***

Research shows that couples that are living in happy and best marriage relationships are those who are the ***masters of dialogue.*** Deciding not to greet, talk or converse with your partner, or not to cook and not to buy her flowers anymore in order to resolve a particular conflict, will never surpass ***the power of dialogue.*** In actual fact, I see dialogue as a form of therapeutic communication when it is done with honesty and genuineness by both partners.

No one wants his or her marriage relationship to be marred by disgraceful conflicts. Dialogue is not an acrimonious debate, however, from time to time couples do experience this kind of debate. Although most arguments and fights between a couple can be resolved, they may be a point where progress seems to be hitting a brick wall.

The biggest challenge to dialogue is withdrawal, where one partner just decides that he or she is not going to be part of any dialogue in the relationship. This brings everything to a ***"stand still"*** mode, as far as working towards finding a solution through conversation is concerned. It is a fact that withdrawal cannot be a long-term solution to relationship challenges, because it leaves the problem unresolved and still waiting for you, as it has not been dealt with in the first place.

The concept of ***objectivity*** is very crucial when managing arguments, this will play out where the ***point of focus is said to be the marriage and not the actions of the couple.*** Let me zoom-in at this concept to make myself clearer. If one spouse likes to buy chicken pies for snacking or one likes to wear socks of dark colours as opposed to bright colours, such actions have no detrimental effect to the marriage. When putting focus on the marriage to see what effect these actions have on it, I will find that they have almost zero effect, then why kick-up a fuss to your spouse about them? The mistake that we often do as couples is to start a squabble over trivial matters. In other words, making a mountain out of a mole hill.

However, let us take examples of actions of infidelity and actions of money problems and then focus on the marriage to see if it is seriously affected by these actions.

The actions will definitely have effect on the marriage and the effect of these actions will be very high. The focal point should be reflecting that. Otherwise, if the point of focus which is the marriage was showing no effect at all by the two actions (infidelity & money problems), then we would not bother about them. In other words, the actions relating to snacking pies and socks will not bother the marriage relationship; but infidelity and money problems will do big time. So, what's the point? Look at the effect of your spouse's actions to the marriage before condemning him or her. If what your spouse is doing does not hurt the marriage, then it's about time you put your egotistical attitudes aside. You may happen to be a bit selfish but without knowing it. Kindly, perhaps you may wish to check that out.

The point here is that one spouse should filter the actions of the other spouse in the light of the actions' effect or impact on their marriage relationship. ***Focusing on the spouse's actions alone without their impact on the marriage relationship may be too personal and selfish. This will be limiting to each other's independence and freedom.*** We should accept the reality that there will be personal preferences and every spouse is entitled to that. The diversity concept explains that each spouse is different and unique. You are uniquely you and your spouse is uniquely himself or herself, that will not change and not anytime soon.

In a dialogue, the partners could spend more time talking about the different solution alternatives other than going into the depths of the problems; then they will enjoy the dialogue. It will be like both of you going into the showroom of the car dealership and looking at the different models of new cars available for your purchase.

Do not blame the marriage counselor when there's a failure to resolve a specific conflict in the marriage by saying, *"The counselor has failed my marriage!"* Every time there's a failure to resolve a marital conflict, the couple should take responsibility for that. The counselor may suggest a process to follow only as a guide but cannot force adults to do what they ought to do. ***The responsibility is on the shoulders of the couple to resolve their problems.*** The Apostle Paul mentions that, each spouse in the marriage relationship has a duty to do things that make the other spouse happy, and he mentions no third party's help in this regard.

To be brutally honest and brutally fair, some husbands are rude and grumpier compared to others; and some wives are stubborn and more offensive compared to others. There is no *"one size fits all"* solution to marriage relationship challenges. So, couples have to constantly and continuously work on their relationships with unfailing passion. To be masters of dialogue is neither easy nor very difficult, ***the couple has to work on it until they master it.*** The secret of it is the willingness and patience to do it by both spouses. Besides, it takes two to tango.

In order to resolve a problem amicably you need to claim your fair share of your responsibility to any problem in the relationship. Check what role you played, what you could have done differently, and what can you do now to contribute positively and meaningfully towards finding a solution. Complete withdrawal is not the perfect solution to the management of arguments in a marriage relationship. As partners in marriage, we still do things that disturb or hurt each other's feelings not by intention and also intentionally.

Do not make any demands when engaging in a dialogue with your partner. Always try to maintain a calm and pleasant situation throughout the conversation. Remember that, boiling water has always a potential to spill over and burn anybody nearby. Reaching an impasse is always a possibility, partners should learn to skillfully park difficult issues one side and deal with the easy wins; and perhaps deal with the difficult ones later when they would have ***"wised-up"*** a little bit. Just have a look at this passage:

"To have lawsuits at all with one another is already a defeat for you. Why not rather suffer wrong? Why not rather be defrauded?"
(1 Cor. 6:7 ESV).

Why not accept the wrong in order to resolve the squabble? This is definitely not an easy thing to do. That is why Paul is posing it as a question, he is not giving an instruction about it and he is not enforcing it, but he throws it in as a suggestion. A good lesson to us as couples is that we shouldn't force difficult decisions on each other, but we should rather throw a suggestion and leave it to the other partner to think about it and decide later what to do.

This has to start as a learning process. One needs to learn to invite and accept ***"Dialogue"*** as a frequent visitor in the relationship. Who knows? Sooner than later Dialogue may happen to swap places with *"Mr & Mrs Frequent Argument"*. As Dialogue takes over as frequent visitor, this may happen until it makes your system its dwelling place. The fact of the matter is that, as a couple you would have internalized it into your system. ***Your mindset needs Dialogue as part of its life skills team.*** You should bear in mind that, couples who are living healthy and happy marriages are the ones who are the masters of dialogue.

When the swapping of places has taken place, *"Mr & Mrs Frequent Argument"* will then become very scarce visitors in the marriage relationship. Remember my plea, I have appealed that you take it easy on each other as a couple when talking about the contents of this book. This is not a book whose contents you should be fighting over. If that happens, please stop immediately right where you are, because dialogue has slipped-off your vocabulary, you need to go back and pick it up. It is a very handy skill in a marriage relationship. It makes the couple to act wisely.

ANALOGY QUIZ: GOOD MANAGEMENT OF ARGUMENTS			
No.	**ASSESSMENT STATEMENTS** (where 10 is most likely and 5 means it needs some tender loving attention)	**10**	**5**
1.	Reality is that arguments are inevitable in a marriage relationship, including ours.		
2.	What is more important is how well we manage them.		
3.	I am good in managing every argument before it gets out of hand.		
4.	My partner is good in managing every argument before it gets out of hand.		
5.	I am unique and I have my personal preferences in the relationship.		
6.	I understand the things that make my partner uniquely unique in our relationship.		
7.	We are the masters of meaningful dialogue in our relationship.		
8.	We take responsibility for all arguments in our relationship.		
9.	Our marriage relationship has never been marred by disgraceful conflicts.		
10.	*"Mr & Mrs Frequent Argument"* are no longer frequent guests in our relationship.		
11.	Dialogue is part of our Mindset's life skills team fulltime.		

12.	Our focus is on what hurts the relationship and not on each other or trivial issues.		
13.	So far we've not even fought over the contents of this book in our dialogue times, we are taking it easy with each other big time.		
14.	In general, how do you rate the overall management of arguments in your marriage relationship now.		
15.	My partner accepts me for who I am including my own preferences, likes and dislikes, and I accept my partner for the person he/she is including his/her own preferences, likes and dislikes.		

Quiz Notes:
The quiz has 15 items, having an overall score of 150 means you are doing just fine in the *"element"* as far as the 15 items are concerned; and there is minimal enhancement or improvement that needs to be done. A score of 135 (90%) means tender loving attention is required on all items with a score of 5. A score of 120 (80%) and below means that quite a bit of work has to be done, because 20% or more of the items have scored 5 points each instead of 10. One may not comfortably say they have mastered or internalized Management of Arguments in their relationship.

One has to do some serious introspection, and then further engage in a meaningful dialogue with the spouse about this. If things seem to be overwhelming, you still have the professional counselor on your side for guidance. Remember, the quiz is not the counselor, it only gives clues as to say, among others, what things you need to consider in your endeavor of improving Good Management of Arguments in your relationship.

CHAPTER 15

WILLINGNESS TO HEAR YOUR PARTNER'S VIEWPOINT

Learn to admire and embrace the beauty of diversity in the marriage relationship, then you won't have a problem why your spouse is so different from you. Avoid being nuisance, where according to Oxford languages dictionary nuisance means a person or thing causing inconvenience or annoyance. No tough talking here, just the explanation of words, right? If you think that's tough language, you ain't heard nothing yet.

A heady and high minded partner is also filled with a lot of ingratitude, I mean a lack of thankfulness and appreciation of what the other partner brings into the relationship. The difference of opinions does not mean you do not love or respect each other; and being in a situation of conflict does not mean the end of the marriage relationship. It means that the relationship has got challenges and there has to be solutions for such challenges. Some solutions are already there but just need to be discovered.

Having difference of opinions can be very much enriching among couples especially when they happen to understand it. Each partner in the relationship has to understand and accept that the other partner has personal views and opinions. Just because you achieved something great does not mean you are better than anyone else in the relationship. Partners should learn to be open-minded persons to each other rather than being close-minded. They should be receptive of each other's ideas about issues in the marriage relationship. The most important aspect here would be the rigidity of the partners versus their flexibility, where the flexibility has to out-weigh the rigidity for the benefit of the relationship.

The *"Peer Pressure"* which is one form of social persuasion is greatly influencing the way married couples make some of their crucial decisions. As part of your dialogue sessions you should include the discussion of ***"submission by the wife"*** versus ***"love by the husband".*** You may be surprised to discover that there are totally two different views or interpretations of submission. Where the female spouse interprets submission differently from the male. This difference of opinions will be what would be at play in the marriage relationship as far as submission by the wife is concerned. It is better to reach consensus on the matter, because agreeing to disagree on this one is not good enough for the relationship; because that may have negative impact on how you resolve areas of conflict in the future.

In my point of view to be honest, agreeing to disagree is not a win-win situation for the partners, because no one has won but you have chosen to remain at *"loggerheads"* and the misunderstanding remains unresolved. Take a look at the following passage;

"[22] Wives, submit to your own husbands, as to the Lord. [23] For the husband is head of the wife, as also Christ is head of the church; and He is the Savior of the body. 24 *Therefore, just as*

the church is subject to Christ, so let the wives be to their own husbands in everything. [25] *Husbands, love your wives, just as Christ also loved the church and gave Himself for her."* (Eph. 5:22-25).

The passage may sound simple as it is, but has also become a very serious and controversial issue practically amongst the married couples; some even before they became married. Others become uncomfortable just by having to discuss it, let alone the practical side of it as implied.

What I came across in life is that there is a secular interpretation of submission by the wife in the marriage relationship, with its own protection by boundaries and limitations having the firm basis on the 50/50 principle. There is also the Biblical interpretation taken verbatim as mentioned by the Holy Writ passage quoted above; with no 50/50 principle to appease the wife not to feel offended, oppressed or enslaved by the requirement of submission to husband. Then the bone of contention starts to emerge.

Somebody told me that it sounds obvious and gentle when the gentleman is asked to love his wife, but it sounds a bit harsh when the wife is asked to submit to her husband in everything. The follow up question from the same person was, *"Where is the choice for the wife?"* Then I realized the existence of different moulds of conventional beliefs in our troubled societies, which are plagued by gender based violence where men have become the main perpetrators.

We have to break some of these moulds for us to have breakthrough to peace and happiness in our marriage relationships. However, breaking these moulds will not be easy because they have been there for decades, it is like breaking down the spiritual strongholds. It will also be like revolutionizing your thinking and decision making process in order to achieve peace and happiness in the marriage relationship.

A woman with a rock-solid relationship with the Most-High God will not stumble or argue against what God is teaching, but she will find a prudent way to adopt that into her life lifestyle. It is also not wise to attack somebody's view as being wrong and rebellious; without understanding where he or she is coming from with his or her belief, even a point of view for that matter.

Acknowledging the fact that we are coming from different backgrounds, it is wise for the partners to engage in a healthy and meaningful dialogue concerning the issue of wife submitting to the husband, and the husband loving the wife. Reaching consensus on this issue is highly beneficial to the relationship. There are those who have gone past this hurdle successfully and with understanding. To be specific, the wife should list and mention the things she thinks she should be doing to show the submission to the husband.

On the other hand, the husband should list and mention the things he thinks the wife should be doing in order to show submission to him. Then the two partners should align and reconcile their expectations concerning submission by the wife. When they happen to reach a consensus on that process, they would have done a great job for themselves and their relationship. The same process stated above will apply to husband loving the wife issue. ***Nothing beats consensus when it comes to dealing with serious and controversial matters between couples.***

This process will also afford you the advantage of understanding some stereotypes that are in existence within each other's mindsets. You should bear in mind that, these stereotypes would definitely be at play every now and then in the marriage relationship. So, it's worth a while to understand them now.

I would like to qualify my discussion by saying that submission in a marriage relationship means selflessness, service from the heart, accountability for all that you do, and respect for your partner, which should also be mutual. It is not some form of justified slavery or a call to woman's abuse. It is very crucial for husbands to understand their authority in the manner of Christ's sacrificial love. Perhaps they should also know that being the head of the house is far from abuse of power or master to slave relationship in a marital union. The fact of the matter is that, when exercising his authority, man ensures the wife's enjoyment of peace, tranquility and security as well as protection from any harm and danger. ***Once the couples understand equality and authority in the relationship, then they will have no issues about submission.***

The partner's viewpoint is the same as the partner's stance or standpoint on a particular issue. Positions like this should be dealt with in respect and caution during the dialogue sessions of the couple. ***When you have become the masters of dialogue as a couple, your conversation on any issue should yield positive results, no matter how sensitive, serious and delicate the issues are***. The other major challenges that hurt marriage relationships are the egotistical attitudes of partners which later culminate into selfishness. I mean a situation where each partner holds his or her own and become very much opinionated; one should bear in mind that, this kind of situation is anti-tranquility in the relationship and that is definitely not what the partners want.

The mentioned situation is also anti-flexibility and when the very opinionated partners are required by the situation to be flexible and bend, they breakdown. As a couple, you need to talk about your flexibility in the relationship; you need to talk about how your egotistical attitudes affect the relationship. You also have to talk about what you need to change to make things better than what they are now.

You should bear in mind that it is not only the relationship that must change, but also the people of the relationship. If they do not change then no positive change or improvement will happen to the relationship. ***Bear in mind that the relationship is reflective of the actions and behaviors of the partners in the relationship.*** The fact of the matter is that ***the relationship has no actions and behavior of its own but that of the partners in the relationship.*** It takes a willing mind and a willing heart to be flexible in the marriage relationship, that's a great sign of humility and commitment.

One partner may have a viewpoint to share, but if the other partner is not willing even to listen, that conversation will not go any further. We all learn to be good listeners and that is a crucial skill that we need to pursue as married couples. It is very disappointing to have something to say to your partner and no one is interested to listen. This element in discussion is very much associated to the element of *"Good Communication & Listening".* These two elements should not be taken lightly because there is a researched fact which states that, ***these have a huge potential to test the marriage relationship to the limits,*** and some marriages have succumbed to that test.

You should be willing to hear, know, understand and value your spouse's viewpoints on matters shared with you. That makes a big difference and boost to your partner's self-esteem and self-worth, that will make him or her a meaningful contributor to the health and survival of the marriage relationship. When you become weak, that is the person who will pick you up, and that is why you should ensure that your partner is always strong through your unwavering support.

ANALOGY QUIZ: WILLINGNESS TO HEAR YOUR PARTNER'S VIEWPOINT			
No.	**ASSESSMENT STATEMENTS** (where 10 is most likely and 5 means it needs some tender loving attention)	**10**	**5**
1.	I am always willing to take time to hear my partner's view points on different matters of life in our relationship.		
2.	My partner is always willing to take time to hear my view points on different matters of life in our relationship.		
3.	I do not force my partner to see things the way I see them.		
4.	My partner does not force me to see things the way he or she sees them.		
5.	I always respect my partner's views when he or she brings them across.		
6.	My partner always respects my views when I bring them across.		
7.	Often times I forsake my own views to accommodate my partner's views.		
8.	Often times my partner forsakes his or her own views to accommodate mine.		
9.	My partner always admires it when I bring in new ideas.		
10.	I always admire it when my partner brings in new ideas.		

11.	My partner is never weary of change when it occurs in our relationship.		
12.	I am never weary of change when it occurs in our relationship.		
13.	My partner's attitude is the booster to my self-esteem. (e.g. confidence/self-trust)		
14.	My attitude is the booster to my partner's self-esteem. (e.g. confidence/self-trust)		
15.	I feel as a recognized meaningful contributor in our marriage relationship.		

Quiz Notes:

The quiz has 15 items, having an overall score of 150 means you are doing just fine in the *"element"* as far as the 15 items are concerned; and there is minimal enhancement or improvement that needs to be done. A score of 135 (90%) means tender loving attention is required on all items with a score of 5. A score of 120 (80%) and below means that quite a bit of work has to be done, because 20% or more of the items have scored 5 points each instead of 10. One may not comfortably say they have mastered or internalized Willingness to Hear Partner's Viewpoint in their relationship.

One has to do some serious introspection, and then further engage in a meaningful dialogue with the spouse about this. If things seem to be overwhelming, you still have the professional counselor on your side for guidance. Remember, the quiz is not the counselor, it only gives clues as to say, among others, what things you need to consider in your endeavor of improving Willingness to Hear Partner's Viewpoint in your relationship.

CHAPTER 16

ABILITY AND WILLINGNESS TO FORGIVE

Every spouse has to learn to be sensitive to the hurts and heartaches that happen in the marriage relationship, in other words, don't act as if nothing is happening to your partner or even to yourself. The wrongs and hurts that we do to each other as a couple are not the same, so is their weight and impact on the wronged spouse. Some of the heartaches may need some time to heal, and such time must be allowed understandably by both spouses to take its course. Keeping grudge has nothing to do with what I'm talking about. One spouse may apologize to the other and be forgiven and peace is made, but the hurt will not vanish or disappear instantly. It will need its time period to heal and the forgiven partner should be sensitive and be positively responsive to that healing process.

The practical example is that of getting a bruise in a fight; and peace may be made between the fighting partners, but the bruise will need to take its time to heal. It cannot just disappear immediately after peace is made. Given all that I have said, the passage below should also be taken into cognizance.

Positive responsiveness to the healing process after the hurt is critical to avoid relapse, and God the Uncreated Creator will do the rest in the process.

What is important and critical to the forgiving spouse is that the spouse must allow the healing of the hurt to take place; just embrace the process and let it take its full course. If you do the contrary you will be delaying the healing and prolonging the hurt and its pain to the wronged and hurting spouse; even after all the repentance, the remorse, the forgiveness and the ***reconciliation have been done. If you are the spouse that is experiencing the hurt, your total healing is what will mean the ultimate peace to you.***

So allow the healing process to take place and do not block or resent it, or you will be extending the unwanted pain. Bear in mind, the marriage must ***survive,*** it must also be ***healthy*** and these two aspects must be sustained. The reason why I'm mentioning the two is that the marriage may be surviving but not healthy, condition wise. You should learn not to interfere with the healing process of your partner, and also that of yourself by doing and saying hurtful things to each other after you have made peace.

"You must be kind to each other. Think of the other person. Forgive other people just as God forgave you because of Christ's death on the cross."
(Eph 4:32 NLV).

"Most important of all, continue to show deep love for each other, for love covers a multitude of sins."
(1 Pet. 4:8).

One spouse has nothing to lose by forgiving the other spouse again and again for the mistakes made in the marriage life. However, there is more to benefit when one spouse forgives the other. You increase and maximize the chances or conditions of marriage survival and sustenance.

You even free-up your very own spirit, you kill the chances of growing apart as a couple; you sustain your spiritual freedom by keeping yourself burden free. You also decrease the chances of ***"relational divergence"*** which is a source of growing apart in the marriage relationship.

"[21]Then Peter came and said to Him, "Lord, how often shall my brother sin against me and I forgive him? Up to seven times?" [22]Jesus said to him, "I do not say to you, up to seven times, but up to seventy times seven."
(Matt. 18:21-22 NSB).

So, go ahead and forgive even a million times as long as God Almighty gives you strength to do it. Having said that, there is one more reality to mention to married couples in this regard; we are all human and we normally get sick and tired of the ***"not so good"*** marriage circumstances created by our partners; time after time. My take on that is that one has to be sick and tired of getting sick and tired when marriage problems come like a flood, ***and should start the golden process of getting to a healthy and meaningful dialogue with the spouse.*** Do it over and over again. It is not easy but it works, so why would one ignore something that works? ***What I mean is that the couple should come and reason together and together they win. Stonewalling is not the real deal for marriage problems.***

Withdrawal is not the perfect answer if it's an answer any way; because running away from a marital problem between you partners will not solve it or take it away. You will always find it where you left it, and sometimes if it's a stubborn one it will also have audacity to follow you wherever you go. It is also a fact that we live our marriage life in cycles where history tends to repeat itself.

Let me say this, ***when you have internalized and mastered the ability and willingness to forgive; you will forgive wholeheartedly even when your partner is not apologizing, and not even interested to apologize.*** It is so amazing how the Lord Jesus Christ, my Best Role Model ever, forgave the wrong doers without expecting any apology from them.

"Then said Jesus, Father, forgive them; for they know not what they do. And they parted his raiment, and cast lots." (Luke 23:34 KJV).

Whilst they were doing Him more harm than good, Christ asked for their forgiveness. He never looked back. I concur with the fact that those couples who turn to stare at their past for so long have their backs turned to their future, thus depriving themselves a good focus to positive things ahead. Behavioral scientists discovered that a narcissist always struggles to forgive. This is a person who has an excessive interest in themselves but disregarding the feelings of others; also referred to as having a personality disorder.

Once you have forgiven and made peace with your partner's *"not so good"* old or recent past, that should never be mentioned again as a fighting issue with your partner. Quoting it in an argument with your partner and follow it up with the words, *"No wonder you are still behaving like this even today"*; that would be a sign of bad relationship in the marriage. That has to change drastically. Perhaps I would say that's an early sign of marriage cancer, but it can be beaten. It takes the will of the affected spouses to do it. ***Your ability and willingness to forgive could bring health and happiness to your marriage.***

Let me also put it this way; if you want to understand the present status of your relationship, you have to analyze and understand what has been in the past. However, do not focus on the past but you should understand it in order to successfully deal with the present. By doing this, you will be empowered to create change, whether in your own life or in somebody else's life such as your spouse.

So, I am of the view that by forgiving your partner, you will be creating change in his or her own life and also in the marriage relationship. You should also know that people are not their bad actions, but they are just trapped in that condition. What I also mean is that ***some people don't just do the things they do just for the reasons we think they do them for.***

We need to go deeper to understand their plight, and we may even find a better reason to forgive them for what they've done towards us. In actual fact, we may have to apologize to them later when we happen to understand their situation versus our stubbornness not to forgive them earlier. How's that? Another crucial factor is that, by giving an evaluative feedback to your partner about his or her wrongs; you will be helping your partner to have control of the wrong behavioral pattern by providing him or her with the possible options available to do that.

This chapter's heading is not saying *"Forgive"* but it says, *"Ability and Willingness to Forgive."* Ability means possession of the means or skill to do something. A man or woman may be willing to forgive but say, *"I just can't find it in myself to forgive, I just cannot do it."* This has nothing to do with physical ability because no physical strength is required here, but we are talking mental and spiritual ability to forgive. There is a way to help and guide somebody to acquire the mental ability and the spiritual ability to forgive willingly and by the power of choice.

Let's now focus on *"Willingness"* for a moment. Willingness is preparedness and readiness to do something, and this is accepted by choice and without reluctance. In terms of this chapter, willingness defines a partner's disposition showing no sense of resentment or hesitation but going for forgiveness, based on the apology of the offending partner. Disposition is the display of a person's inherent qualities of mind and character. In other words, it is the mentality and frame of mind about a certain position taken. So, my take is that, if your willingness to forgive emanates from your disposition with a touch of ability in it, it is bound to work and yield positive results.

This is not just playing with words; because it is possible to be willing to forgive and yet stumble on the ability to do it. Hence I found *"Ability and Willingness to Forgive"* to a be meaningful heading for this chapter.

I would also like to mention that, if you are a staunch Christian like myself, you may wish to link the issue of *"Ability and Willingness to Forgive"* to compliance with Christian principles associated with this topic. These may include;

- The Lord's prayer, "Father forgive our sins as we forgive those who sin against us."
- The Lord's teaching, "Forgiving each other seventy times seven."
- Repenting in order to be forgiven – (2 Cor. 7:10-12).

Always get yourself into the process of being able and willing to forgive your partner. When you have internalized that, you will never look back again on things you've forgiven him or her on.

ANALOGY QUIZ: ABILITY AND WILLINGNESS TO FORGIVE

No.	ASSESSMENT STATEMENTS (where 10 is most likely and 5 means it needs some tender loving attention)	10	5
1.	I always have the ability and willingness to forgive my partner.		
2.	My partner always has the ability and willingness to forgive me.		
3.	I always allow time for the healing process when I forgive or being forgiven by my spouse.		
4.	My partner always allows time for the healing process when he/she has forgiven me or being forgiven by myself.		
5.	I don't count how many times I have forgiven my partner or my partner has forgiven me.		
6.	My partner doesn't count how many times he/she has forgiven me or my partner has been forgiven by myself.		
7.	I always make peace when I forgive my partner and never look back.		
8.	My partner always makes peace when he/she forgives me and never looks back.		
9.	I provide my partner with evaluative feedback on his/her wrongs and possible options to consider for change, in addressing the wrong behavioral pattern.		

10.	My partner provides me with evaluative feedback on my wrongs and possible options to consider for change, in addressing my wrong behavioral pattern.		
11.	Oftentimes I apologize to my partner for being stubborn and not forgiving on time.		
12.	Oftentimes my partner apologizes to me for being stubborn and not forgiving me on time.		
13.	My ability and willingness to forgive my partner is being tested several times by my partner's willingness to apologize, and I always pass the test.		
14.	My partner's ability and willingness to forgive me is being tested several times by my willingness to apologize, my partner always passes the test.		
15.	I have the ability and willingness to forgive wholeheartedly even when my partner is not interested to apologize to me.		
16.	I can honestly say that I have internalized the process of being able and willing to forgive my partner in various aspects of our marriage relationship.		

Quiz Notes:

The quiz has 16 items, and having an overall score of 160 means you are doing just fine in this *"element"* as far as the 16 items are concerned; and there is minimal enhancement or improvement that needs to be done. Any score below 144 (90%) means that tender loving attention is required on all items that score a 5. A score of 80 (50%) and below means that one has to do a lot of work to reach confidence level on this *"element"*. One has to do some serious introspection, and then further engage in a meaningful dialogue with the spouse. If things seem to be overwhelming, you still have the professional counselor on your side for guidance. Remember, the quiz is not the counselor, it only gives clues as to say, among others, what things you need to consider on your way to making your marriage happy as far as the element of Ability and Willingness to Forgive is concerned.

CHAPTER 17

WILLINGNESS TO APOLOGIZE

It normally works better for the relationship and for the sake of achieving the ultimate reconciliation, if the spouse who has realized to be on the wrong side initiates reconciliation by showing remorse and asks forgiveness. This should be done with the earnest honesty and without any form of arrogance or self-justification. You need to show remorse when you apologize to your partner, otherwise your apology may not be as meaningful as it should be to him or her.

What is apology? It is a deep regret or guilt for a wrong committed or an expression of regret for something that one has done wrong. Often times as married couples we find ourselves on the wrong side in our marriage relationships, and by so doing we offend our partners. The apple of discord comes when we have to humble ourselves and remorsefully apologize by saying, *"I'm sorry."* Let's quickly define remorse because it is very key in the process of apologizing.

"Remorse is a distressing emotion experienced by an individual who regrets actions which they have done in the past that they deem to be shameful, hurtful, or wrong. Remorse is closely allied to guilt and self-directed resentment." (Wikipedia). My take is that, remorse brings more weight in your act of apologizing. That extra heaviness weighs down on your spouse's heart such that it becomes unbearable for him or her not to forgive you. So, don't take

remorse lightly, it is very heavy on the heart. Yes, it has that magic touch which could tip the scale of your partner's heart.

Note that the chapter heading is not saying ***"Apologize"*** but it says, ***"Willingness to Apologize."*** Let's focus on ***"Willingness"*** for a moment. Willingness is preparedness and readiness to do something, and this is accepted by choice and without reluctance. In terms of this chapter willingness defines a partner's disposition showing no sense of resentment or hesitation but going for apology. Disposition is the display of your partner's inherent qualities of mind and character. In other words, it is the mentality and frame of mind about a certain position taken. So, my take is that, if your apology emanates from your disposition with a touch of remorse in it, it is bound to work and yield positive results.

I would also like to mention that, if you are a staunch Christian like myself, you may wish to link the issue of ***"Willingness to Apologize"*** to compliance with Christian principles associated with this topic. These may include;

- Repenting in order to be forgiven – (2 Cor. 7:10-12).
- ***"If another believer sins against you, go privately and point out the offense. If the other person listens and confesses it, you have won that person back."*** (Matt. 18:15 NLT).
- ***"Confess your sins to each other and pray for each other so that you may be healed. The earnest prayer of a righteous person has great power and produces wonderful results."*** (James 5:16 NLT).

Please hear me correctly, I do not rule out that the wronged partner can initiate reconciliation by accepting the wrong he or she has not done, for the sake of peace in the marriage.

However, if that be the case, there are many chances than not, that the partner on the wrong side of things may continue on the wrong side oftentimes. He or she may even repeat the wrongs committed sometimes, perhaps without recognizing any wrong doing from his or her side.

When guilt acceptance eventually overcomes denial and pride, that sets a good platform for a real and true reconciliation, and peace to take place and prevail. This should be thoroughly understood by each spouse, especially the one who happens to be on the wrong side of things. ***This is very fundamental to any true reconciliation in a marriage relationship.***

Let me deviate for a moment to prison, prisoners and their coming back to the society. Research finding states that the more the time that prisoners serve in their sentences behind bars; the lesser are their chances of successful rehabilitation back into the society; and the more likely that they will re-offend after they come out of prison.

Just on that part of the research alone, the married couples should learn that ***it is not good for the survival and sustenance of the marriage to remain on the wrong for a long time, because the wrong done constantly may become a new internalized normal in the marriage relationship.***

"Be angry, yet do not sin." Do not let the sun set upon your anger,"
(Eph. 4:26 BSB).

"... for man's anger does not bring about the righteousness that God desires."
(James 1:20 BSB).

The Lesson is that do not hesitate or procrastinate, always work swiftly towards reconciliation. Buy no time because that may cost you your marriage relationship. I know this may be easier said than done, but you should be constantly conscious about it and constantly be working towards it. You should not be doing nothing about it, because that is where the danger lies. We are all accountable for the decisions we take.

Using gestures to apologize to your partner is not enough. You need to say it, *"Honey, I'm sorry for doing one, two and three".* Do it by your own mouth by telling it to your spouse's ears and looking at his or her eyes, and the least is to send a message to your spouse. Sending her flowers is not enough or cooking him his best meal is also not enough. The flowers and the meal cannot and say, *"I'm sorry"*, they have their own language which they purposefully serve, but they cannot show remorse. You need to engage in a dialogue with your spouse, ***because the wronged spouse needs to hear some answers and not flowers or a nice cooked meal.***

Remember, God needed some answers from Adam and Eve when they breached His conditions of living in the Garden of Eden.

"Who told you that you were naked?" the LORD God asked. "Have you eaten from the tree whose fruit I commanded you not to eat?"
(Gen. 3:11 NLT).

The parable of the repentant prodigal son was also made for a purpose, and we can learn a lot from that as married couples. (Luke 15:11-32). Look at his disposition, way before he even approached his father. Look at him at the time he was watching the pigs feeding, and that was the time his disposition emerged concerning the decision about his situation. We all know what he said and the decision he took and with a touch of remorse in it, it worked well for him. ***Regardless of his condition, the disposition of the prodigal son taught us a great lesson for our marriage relationships. You should always learn to apologize for your mistakes to your partner, but don't forget that touch of remorse in your apologies.***

ANALOGY QUIZ: WILLINGNESS TO APOLOGIZE			
No.	**ASSESSMENT STATEMENTS** (where 10 is most likely and 5 means it needs some tender loving attention)	**10**	**5**
1.	I am always willing to apologize to my partner when I have wronged him or her.		
2.	My partner is always willing to apologize to me when he or she is in the wrong.		
3.	I am always prepared to apologize even if I'm not the one who is wrong.		
4.	My partner apologizes even if he or she is not the one who is wrong but me.		
5.	Willingness and Apology are part of practical fundamentals in our marriage.		
6.	There is nothing that can stand in front of my willingness to apologize, even my anger.		
7.	There is nothing that can stand in front of my partner's willingness to apologize, even his or her anger.		
8.	Stubbornness and arrogance are weak compared by my willingness to apologize and my partner knows it.		
9.	Stubbornness and arrogance are weak compared by my partner's willingness to apologize and I know it.		
10.	I always remain willing to apologize even when my partner is not apologizing.		

11.	My partner always remains willing to apologize even when I am not apologizing.		
12.	I always accept guilt and overcome denial and pride, and my partner knows it.		
13.	My partner always accepts guilt and thus overcomes denial and pride.		
14.	I always show remorse when apologizing to my partner.		
15.	My partner always shows remorse when apologizing to me.		
16.	Regardless of his condition, the disposition of the prodigal son taught me a great lesson for our marriage relationship.		
17.	I understand that gestures cannot be remorseful, I need to apologize directly to my partner and he or she needs to hear some answers from me.		
18.	I always forgive my partner but also tell him or her not to stay in the wrong for long.		
19.	My partner always forgives me but also tells me not to stay in the wrong for long.		
20.	We have already mastered and internalized "Willingness to Apologize" in our marriage relationship.		

Quiz Notes:
The quiz has 20 items, having an overall score of 200 means you are doing just fine in the *"element"* as far as the 20 items are concerned; and there is minimal enhancement or improvement that needs to be done. A score of 180 (90%) means tender loving attention is required on all items with a score of 5. A score of 160 (80%) and below means that quite a bit of work has to be done, because 20% or more of the items have scored 5 points each instead of 10. One may not comfortably say they have mastered or internalized Willingness to Apologize in their relationship.

One has to do some serious introspection, and then further engage in a meaningful dialogue with the spouse about this. If things seem to be overwhelming, you still have the professional counselor on your side for guidance. Remember, the quiz is not the counselor, it only gives clues as to say, among others, what things you need to consider in your endeavor of improving Willingness to Apologize in the relationship.

CHAPTER 18

SHOWING EMPATHY, SYMPATHY AND RESPONSIVENESS

SHOWING EMPATHY

In line with the Oxford languages dictionary, in a marriage relationship ***Empathy*** can be defined as the ability of one partner to understand and share the feelings of the another partner. It is also defined as the ability to accurately put yourself *"in someone else's shoes".* This involves understanding the other partner's situation, perceptions and feelings from their point of view; and be able to communicate that understanding back to your partner.

The opposite of that is apathy which is defined as a lack of interest, enthusiasm and concern; and apathy is one word that the couple should not have in their relationship's vocabulary. Empathy has emotional healing effects since it is therapeutic by characterization. It is a unique human ability to share the emotions of your partner. This is a critical skill for you to have as a marriage partner.

The Cambridge dictionary defines *Therapeutic* as causing someone to feel happier and more relaxed or to be healthy. So, ***empathy is a characteristic of a therapeutic communication in a relationship.*** Ruthless and heartless can only be the opposites to this wonderful element. Empathy also involves getting into your partner's shoes, opening the conversation and trying to understand what's troubling him or her. This is very much connected to love because love is compassionate and empathetic.

Empathy can be classified as communicable in verbal and nonverbal ways. Whether verbal or nonverbal, empathy can be regarded as one of the qualities of compassionate love. The reason being, it makes someone to take action and do something for someone that he or she compassionately loves. I mean the action that you feel from within and then you act it out.

Nonverbal Empathy

- This means being there in person for your spouse and sitting next to him or her during the time of need such as when the partner is sick, suffered a bereavement on his or her side of the family, losing a job, suffered a financial blow or involved in a motor car accident.

- Showing some active listening when involved in a serious conversation with your spouse. Allowing your partner to talk more by talking less and listening more whilst keeping the eye contact.

- When this happens your spouse is more likely to feel that he or she is being lifted out of the difficult situation by the help of your empathic behavior.

- Showing emotional support to your partner after having a bad day, knowing the fact that all of us are living in this imperfect and troublesome world, where things don't always go our way every day.

- Remember that you are also listening to connect with your partner in spite of the condition and prevailing circumstances.

Verbal Empathy

- This involves making some empathic statements to your partner, which will strengthen and improve the relationship; and the bonding will also become galvanized.

Lack of empathy contributes to the deterioration in the marriage relationship quality over time, whereas, focusing on being empathic will just do the opposite big time. Empathy also reflects the warmth of love in the marriage relationship, if love has run cold the likelihood is that the acts of empathy would be minimal; and it would be difficult to be empathetic under such circumstances.

Empathy enables you to connect to the heart feelings of your partner. Lack of empathy is the result of having a low emotional intelligence, and does not understand the emotions of others including those of your spouse. The fact of the matter is that one partner does not get what the other partner is feeling, therefore, it is not possible to place oneself in another partner's shoes. The reality is that empathy helps the couple to understand each other, and that assists them to build a friendship based on positive relationship of trust. ***You need to understand that enduring commitment is also born out of empathy.*** In actual fact, ***compassion is empathy in action.*** It is that commitment of doing something about the partner's situation which relieves your partner's suffering.

SHOWING SYMPATHY

On the other hand, ***Sympathy*** involves the showing of kindness and understanding to the plight of one spouse by the other; one partner shows the feeling of being sorry for the other in the other's predicament. In the instance where you've even warned your partner before the untoward happened, do not say, ***"I told you!"***. It is a bit late for that now, all you need to do is to support him or her by showing sympathy for the unfortunate situation. As a partner in marriage, strive to be a very strong empath among other great empaths for your partner.

I cannot over-emphasize the importance of learning this crucial skill. When you've mastered it you will be able to see symbolism in various situations. You will look in your marriage, church, family, business, life and the world around you and understand the deeper meaning of their context. This great skill will also allow you to disengage from the subtleties of the situation and circumstances and deal with real issues that need attention. In other words, you become a visionary.

This also gives you the ability to see the good in other people including your spouse, and that is one of the ways you can make change happen. Bear in mind, there is greatness embedded in each and every one of us. You should always remember that you are not an emotionless robot, but you are human and you will need that human connection; so that you can become responsive to your partner's feelings whether good or bad, inward or outward.

SHOWING RESPONSIVENESS

This element is defined as the quality of reacting quick enough and positively to the immediate and long term needs of your partner. It also depicts the ability of either partner to adjust to changes in the internal and external environments, in order to accommodate the other partner in the interest of the marriage relationship. Responsiveness may include taking actions to make your partner happy or taking actions that will protect your spouse and relationship from abuse, harm and danger.

Being responsive is also defined as an attribute of empathy, where a person shows the ability to understand and appreciate the other partner. It is like saying to your partner, ***"I understand that you are rightfully different from me, that is why I am allowing you in the relationship to be who you are."*** Often times as a couple, each one of you should learn and practice to use words that are kind to one another. I have seen a lot of this in practice where partners will call each other sweetheart, honey, my love, baby, etc. This practice also blends nicely with this principle of responsiveness.

Each partner should appreciate transparency of the other as a good personal value, and not take advantage of it. Perhaps, I would say that the element of responsiveness is also reflective of the warmth of compassionate love in the marriage relationship. This element is also regarded as one of the qualities of compassionate love just like empathy and sympathy. As a partner in a marriage relationship, you should never fail to understand that, even the good little things coming from your partner reveal the greatness which you do not see for now. Please appreciate them as they come.

ANALOGY QUIZ: SHOWING EMPATHY, SYMPATHY AND RESPONSIVENESS			
No.	**ASSESSMENT STATEMENTS** (where 10 is most likely and 5 means it needs some tender loving attention)	**10**	**5**
1.	I have a better understanding of my partner's thinking and feelings.		
2.	My partner has a better understanding of my thinking and feelings.		
3.	We respect each other's needs and feelings in the relationship and respond to them accordingly.		
4.	We fully understand and value Responsiveness in our marriage relationship.		
5.	My partner knows that I am responsive in our relationship.		
6.	I know that my partner is showing responsiveness in our relationship.		
7.	My partner goes all out to protect me and our relationship from abuse, harm and danger.		
8.	I go all out to protect my partner and our relationship from abuse, harm and danger.		
9.	My partner is not secretive but transparent to me and I know it.		
10.	I am not secretive but transparent to my partner and he or she knows it.		

11.	My needs to my partner do not get to deaf ears and resentment often times.		
12.	My partner's needs to me do not get to deaf ears and resentment often times.		
13.	In our relationship, transparency is not taken advantage of, but is respected by both of us.		
14.	Often times we call each other using love relationship names like sweetheart, honey, babes, etc.		
15.	My partner is always fast enough to come to my assistance and rescue in times of need.		
16.	I am always fast enough to come to assistance and rescue for my partner in times of need.		
17.	My partner senses it on time when I am depressed and acts accordingly to accommodate me.		
18.	I quickly sense it on time when my partner is depressed and I act accordingly to accommodate him or her.		
19.	My partner never takes advantage of my transparency to him or her.		
20.	I never take advantage of my partner's transparency to me.		

Quiz Notes:
The quiz has 20 items, having an overall score of 200 means you are doing just fine in the *"element"* as far as the 20 items are concerned; and there is minimal enhancement or improvement that needs to be done. A score of 180 (90%) means tender loving attention is required on all items with a score of 5. A score of 160 (80%) and below means that quite a bit of work has to be done, because 20% or more of the items have scored 5 points each instead of 10. One may not comfortably say they have internalized some skills when dealing with Showing Empathy, Sympathy and Responsiveness in their relationship.

One has to do some serious introspection, and then further engage in a meaningful dialogue with the spouse about this. If things seem to be overwhelming, you still have the professional counselor on your side for guidance. Remember, the quiz is not the counselor, it only gives clues as to say, among others, what things you need to consider in your endeavor of improving Showing Empathy, Sympathy and Responsiveness in the relationship.

CHAPTER 19

PRAYING TOGETHER

The old saying says that, *"The family that prays together, stays together."* This sounds truer than not. It is a good thing to often pray together as a couple. Hear me correctly, I do not rule out the private quiet time and devotions individually with God, that is also critical for your spiritual welfare and growth. Each of these things plays an important part in your personal lives and your marriage relationship, oh yes, they do and big time.

The other aspect is that the weapons of our warfare are not carnal, that gives me reason why when I talk about marriage relationships, I do not limit myself to the secular view; because the enemies that attack the marriage relationships are not only secular, there are spiritual enemies too.

Below are some of the reasons why I believe praying together is also good and beneficial to the marriage relationship;

- You learn to understand each other's prayer lists.
- You learn to understand the things that spiritually concern your partner.
- You also learn to understand the things that spiritually uplift your partner.

- You get an opportunity to express yourself how you think and feel about your partner before God whilst your partner is listening.
- You both get the chance to pray about your marriage relationship in the presence of each other.

I am of the view that this is very therapeutic (has some healing effects) to both parties in the relationship, and if it does, God should be ok with it. For an example; the following might be a part of a prayer of a man praying to God whilst his wife is also kneeling next to him and listening;

"Bless my one and only wife, Father God."

"She is the best person that ever came into my life, Lord."

"Even though she may be disrespectful to me at times; but she washes and irons my clothes Lord God, bless her."

"She may be rude, shout and swear at me; but she cooks for me Heavenly Father."

"I love her and I know she loves me and you; and both us love you Father God."

"Lord I believe our marriage is a marriage from you and you alone. Please bless it. Amen."

What I'm trying to say is that a partner will voice out before God what he has inside of him about his partner, as well as the marriage relationship itself. In real terms, you are letting God to know about your heart-beat as far as your marriage relationship is concerned; whilst the other marriage partner is listening. There will be the good and the not so good things, but they are all part of the marriage relationship. The fact of the matter is that you are being honest before God and your partner.

This might become emotional at times where the praying partner runs out of words as a result of emotions, and may start praying in tongues or even crying as part of the prayer language. That's fine but even better to later calm down and start praying again in an understandable language to both partners. I think it is ok for one partner to know how the other partner prays.

This kind of engagement pushes the too relaxed and unconcerned mood away, such that partners start to take their marriage relationship seriously as they should. I do not say that the marriage relationship must always be tense and serious. The couple has to understand that when the relationship has gone too casual; the spiritual side has the power to bring the required seriousness back into the relationship because it also involves God in it. King Solomon said, *"The fear of the Lord is the beginning of Wisdom."* (Proverbs 9:10). So, the spiritual side of the relationship also makes you to wise-up a little bit in the way you do things as a couple.

In the process of praying together you will learn to understand each other's prayer life. Please, do not be judgmental by being fault-finding and condemnatory in the process as you discover your partner's weaknesses; no one is perfect, ***we are all work-in progress in some areas.*** This should be your good opportunity to pray for your partner's weaknesses as you discover them. Believe me you, both of you will be amongst the strongest prayer warriors that stand in the presence of the Most-High God by day and by night.

This will be part of the highlights of your spiritual life as a couple. In my honest opinion this should be very much enriching and fulfilling to a couple. That is why I strongly believe that you should never neglect this spiritual side of the marriage relationship or else, your relationship will not be balanced. I am a firm believer of the balanced life concept, especially in the marriage relationship.

Let me further say this from God's creation point of view, ***"Remember that, as a human being, you were spiritual before you became natural, so why would you neglect the spiritual side when you are now natural? It does not make sense."*** You need to balance your life and relationship with each other and God; because ***a life and a relationship without God remains imbalanced, skewed and found wanting. The spiritual side is key to balancing the scale of the marriage relationship.*** For an example; it is the spiritual side that will give you the added strength to forgive your spouse when he or she has not even cared to apologize to you, after all the wrongs done towards you.

In saying this I do not undermine the good effects of professional counseling, but bear in mind, that has its own limitations too. ***What man can do cannot be compared to what God can directly do to your marriage relationship. Prayer changes things, prayer changes conditions and circumstances. Prayer changes lives and prayer can change you and your partner to the new you, and even better than what both of you have even imagined or seen on each other before. Prayer can guide you to newness and freshness in the marriage relationship, to new wife and new husband as far as personal characters are concerned.*** That is the effect of what the spiritual side can do to a marriage relationship, it should not be neglected or taken for granted at any point in time.

When we pray to God as most Christians do, it is not only about receiving or sustaining the good things we have. It is also about losing, I mean losing the things attached to us which we do not need. Let me explain myself, after much consultation with his or her God through prayer, a spouse should be able to say, ***"I have lost my depression, insecurity, anger, greed, lying and even fear of death."*** So, in our marriage relationships also, let us not only look on the good things we can get, but also on the loses we need to incur. ***The things we do not need are obviously the things we need to lose,*** and by choice and God's help, this is possible.

Religion cannot be divorced from morality. Never ever tell God to get out of your life, to back-off and leave you alone. Only a fool can do that, because the beginning of all wisdom is to reverence the Lord, the uncreated Creator of the Milky Way and the Galaxies, Heaven and the Earth. When one partner hurts the other, he or she is not only hurting the partner, but also himself or herself plus the relationship. So, it is better to stop the foolishness of intentionally hurting one another. The devil and his demons are on the rampage (moving through the world in a violent and uncontrollable manner) destroying marriage relationships. We need to be praying more than before as couples.

Allow me to go further and expatiate on this matter. Nobody else should be going on the knees before God and pray for your partner more than you do. The idea is that every time you open your mouth and heart before the Most-High God, you should not end that session without mentioning your partner in one way or the other in the prayer. The same applies if you have children.

This does not mean that one should not pray for other people and other things that need prayer, but charity begins at home so to speak. If you don't pray for your partner as often as you should, chances are slim for someone else to do it for you. ***Each spouse should pray for the other like no one else could do, make it impossible to finish a session with God without putting your spouse and children before Him.***

If that sounds boring, please bore God with it because He delights to hear your ***"boring"*** prayers if that be the case. God knows what we need but He still wants us to pray to Him. Just like your child, you know the child needs a sandwich but the child must still ask for it, and then you will make a sandwich for the child.

The fact of the matter is that no one knows your partner more than you do. You know things about your partner that the other person doesn't know, and that is why I say that you are the one who is better placed to pray for your partner more than anybody else. Please get me right, I do not disregard other people's prayers for your spouse; but no one can present him or her before God like you. Let praying together find its rightful place in your marriage relationship.

So, please do your part the best way you can and may God bless you.

ANALOGY QUIZ: PRAYING TOGETHER			
No.	**ASSESSMENT STATEMENTS** (where 10 is most likely and 5 means it needs some tender loving attention)	**10**	**5**
1.	There is respect and fear of the Lord in our marriage relationship.		
2.	We always pray together as a couple.		
3.	I know the prayer life of my partner.		
4.	My partner knows my prayer life.		
5.	I believe that praying together strengthens our marriage relationship.		
6.	I probably have a good idea of what features frequently in my partner's prayer list.		
7.	My partner probably has a good idea of what features frequently in my prayer list.		
8.	In my own private prayer I include some of my partner's prayer items to support him by also bringing them before the Most-High God.		
9.	I never miss praying for my partner every time I talk with God alone.		
10.	I like praying to God for my partner while my partner is listening. (shouldn't be shy).		
11.	My partner likes praying to God about me while I listen. (shouldn't be shy).		

12.	I think I'm praying for my partner more than anyone else does.		
13.	Praying together has found its rightful place in our marriage relationship.		
14.	No one knows my partner more than I do.		
15.	No one knows me more than my partner.		
16.	In our marriage relationship we never tell God to back-off and leave us alone, we need Him to be part of our lives.		
17.	I can pin point the good effects of prayer in our marriage relationship.		
18.	Concerning our prayer life in the relationship, my partner and I are strong prayer warriors.		
19.	Both of us understand that our weapons of warfare to protect our marriage relationship should not be carnal.		
20.	We understand that there are things we need to lose in our marriage relationship which are still attached to us. (they should go).		
21.	We do not take for granted the life changing power of prayer in our relationship.		
22.	I find it therapeutic to hear my partner praying for me before the Most-High God.		

23.	We are active members of the prayer support group in our local church.		

Quiz Notes:
The quiz has 23 items, having an overall score of 230 means you are doing just fine in the *"element"* as far as the 23 items are concerned; and there is minimal enhancement or improvement that needs to be done. Keep up the good work. A score of 210 (91%) means tender loving attention is required on all items with a score of 5. A score of 185 (80%) and below means that quite a bit of work has to be done, because 20% or more of the items have scored 5 points each instead of 10. One may not comfortably say they have mastered or internalized Praying Together in their relationship.

One has to do some serious introspection, and then further engage in a meaningful dialogue with the spouse about this. If things seem to be overwhelming, you still have the professional counselor on your side for guidance. Remember, the quiz is not the counselor, it only gives clues as to say, among others, what things you need to consider in your endeavor of improving Praying Together in the relationship.

CHAPTER 20

THE PARAMOUNT CHALLENGE

This is a chapter that is totally different from the elements but it is worth reading for your information and upliftment. Personal levitation is something that we will always need. According to Oxford languages dictionary, paramount means ***"more important than anything else."*** It also means something that is *"having supreme power above other things"* concerning your life. This chapter tries to unpack what that paramount thing could be in a person's life. This could also mean different things to different people depending on the individual's convictions, and also what one's conscience is saying to him or her.

Having gone through the chapters about the elements of good and happy marriages and understood them, and further committed to improve on each of them; that does not become the absolute for the married couples. This chapter says, in addition to knowing and committing to the elements, there's something more that the couples still need to do; and that becomes the paramount challenge to them if they are not doing it already.

To the wife, remember, when your husband proposed, you accepted and then the marriage followed just from that humble commitment. But the important part I'm coming to here is that, from your side you matched that commitment with equal reciprocity. That's what makes the marriage a good and beautiful thing. Hence my question, *"How can one hurt a thing this good?"*

On a similar way the Most-High God is putting a paramount challenge to every human heart today. Just listen to this as you read it loud for your inner ears to hear;

"By his divine power, God has given us everything we need for living a godly life. We have received all of this by coming to know him, the one who called us to himself by means of his marvelous glory and excellence."
(2 Peter 1:3 NLT).

As you read it, these promises are not for sale, you don't have to pay even a cent to receive them. Another version explains the same passage this way;

"His divine power <u>has given us everything we need for life and godliness</u> through the knowledge of Him who called us by His own glory and excellence."
(2 Peter 1:3 BSB).

God declares in Isaiah 45:21-22 that, He is God alone and there is no one else. The apostle Paul states that, *"you can do nothing against the truth, but for the truth."* (2 Cor. 13:8). In actual fact, ***the truth is undisputable.***

Taking a glance at the contemporary situation, people continue to do wrong things according to the desires of their flesh continually until that becomes a new normal in their lives. This is what becomes a problem with God, and that is what happened in Genesis. God had enough of it and He gave the human kind a time slot to repent and later destroyed them with flood when they did not repent from their bad ways of living. Another factor grossly affecting relationships is scriptural disobedience and spiritual laziness, and most of the so called Christians have become secular in terms of behavior and lifestyle.

Every adulterous generation will have to answer to the Almighty God for their sins. I'm not trying to judge anyone or making anyone scared but I'm just stating a Biblical fact which is worthy of consideration. As Christians, we are heirs of God the Almighty and joint heirs with Christ. Whatever God is rich of; we are heirs to that. So, if God is rich in mercy we are heirs to that. So, we ought to be merciful towards our partners and forgive them too.

If God is the God of love, we ought to love our partners unconditionally as God did to us. When we were sinful He said, *"Come to me all you who are weary and heavy laden and I will give you rest."* Let us embrace our partners even when they are stressful and tired because of the toils and struggles of life, when they are neglecting us let us not push them away but embrace them.

The real heir of God has the mind of Christ, because Christ did what the Heavenly Father wanted in the midst of adversity. So, if we are joint heirs with Him we ought to do what the Heavenly Father wants in our marriage relationships no matter the circumstances. ***Remember, you can do what God says you can do and you can be what God says you can be. So, do the best you can do and be the best that you can be.***

Listen to the big question that Jesus once asked His disciples one day. Then he asked them, *"But who do you say I am?"* (Matt. 16:15 NLT).

Who do you say Christ is to your life? Who do you say He is to your marriage relationship? Can you relate Him to your lifestyle or is He not featuring at all?

I fully subscribe to the view that human-kind's dual purpose on earth is:

1.) Knowing God first and then,

2.) Making God known to others.

So, you need to know Him personally before you even make Him known to others. Everything that we need such as healing when we are sick or solutions to our marital challenges; as far as God is concerned that is a done deal. He won't even sweat to make things happen in your life. It takes a matter of faith from our side to effectuate and materialize what we need from Him.

" [6]But he must ask in faith, without doubting, because he who doubts is like a wave of the sea, blown and tossed by the wind. [7]That man should not expect to receive anything from the Lord. [8]He is a double-minded man, unstable in all his ways." (James 1:6-8 BSB). So, if you don't have faith expect nothing from God. The reality is that, what pleases God is having faith in His Word.

"Daughter," said Jesus, "your faith has healed you. Go in peace and be free of your affliction." (Mark 5:34NLT). The Lord Jesus never said, "I have healed you." But He said that it was her faith that healed her.

Faith can make things happen for us. That is as far as Christ is concerned. That's the reason why I regard faith as *"The Substance of Hope and the Evidence of Sight".*

God's messenger to the gentiles once said, *"The weapons of our warfare are not carnal, but they are mighty through God to the pulling down of the strongholds."* (2 Cor. 10:4). That is why I believe that faith cannot be carnal. Even John the elder said, *"Whatever is born of God overcomes the world."* (1John 5:4).

So, if faith is born of God, then it is the *"Super Sense"* in you that will overcome the world and its challenges. However, you have to listen to this first, *"Faith cometh by hearing and hearing by the word of God."* (Rom. 10:17). Let's go a little bit further and deeper on this subject of the super sense.

"... But when the Son of Man returns, how many will he find on the earth who have faith?" (Luke 18:8 NLT).

The biggest challenge that has faced every generation on earth is unbelief, even our modern day generation has not escaped that. The human beings have five natural senses to make contact with the world around them, and these are good and are from God. These are; Hearing, Sight, Smell, Touch and Taste. When you become a Christian by believing God and His word, you have added the sixth sense which is faith, so faith becomes the super sense and without it no one can please God. This is what the enemy attacks. ***Everything from God is received by faith.*** Your faith must grow to be strong, it must be immovable by the enemy. Seek God by faith! Walk with God by faith! and Serve God by Faith!

Faith is called the *"Super Sense"* because it takes over and control the other five natural senses, more especially when those are caught between the wall and the hard place by the challenges of life. That means when the natural senses have exhausted their limits with failure to overcome whatever challenge that was being faced at a point in time. The faith that I am talking about is the faith that you have in God which will control and guide what you choose to hear, see, smell, touch and taste. ***Faith is the weapon that Christians have to use in their spiritual warfare*.**

"For we are not fighting against flesh-and-blood enemies, but against evil rulers and authorities of the unseen world, against mighty powers in this dark world, and against evil spirits in the heavenly places."
(Ephesians 6:12 NLT).

If we are facing these kinds of enemies, how can we limit ourselves to carnality? If we do, our carnal approach alone will never make it against these enemies because they are more advanced than carnality. It is true that our marriage relationships will also face spiritual attacks from the unseen world. When evil spirits attack a marriage relationship, chances will be slim if any for a secular professional counselor to deal with that successfully. I do not think professional marriage counselors in the secular world, have been trained and equipped to deal with the enemies mentioned in the passage above.

It will take your faith in God Almighty and the support from people of like-precious-faith for you to overcome these kinds of enemies, when they attack you and your marriage relationship. Please understand me, I do not rule out help from professional counselors, they play an important role and they are also effective in what they do. However, they are human and they also have limitations especially when it comes to matters mentioned in the verses above. God's paramount challenge to you is to believe in Him for your life. He's challenging you to have a rock-solid relationship with

Him, and not just for a moment but He points it to eternity. That is forever so to speak. What He also means is that your life is incomplete without Him.

Talking about this deep mystery of faith which is much more than a spiritual emotion; four times the Holy Writ states that patriarch Abraham believed God and was counted a righteous person. What was it that Abraham believed? When we find out what Abraham believed, then, we too can be counted as righteous, but only if we choose to believe it. We too can be reconciled and become acceptable to the Most-High God. I mean you can have peace with God whilst living your life and He can be at peace with you.

"And Abram believed the LORD, and the LORD counted him as righteous because of his faith."
(Gen. 15:6 NLT).

What I also learnt in patriarch Abraham's story is that, the Most-High God made a covenant with Abraham because He loved him, and not because Abraham deserved it. The reason being that Abraham's own self-righteousness was just like filthy rags before the Almighty God. ***A relationship lesson here is that we should care, forgive, accept and accommodate our spouses not because they need to deserve it; but it should be because of the compassionate love we have for them even when they do not even deserve it.***

What I mean is that, our partners' self-righteousness may happen not to make it according to our own egotistical and self-centered thinking; but the compassionate love we have for them qualifies them to make it for our care and forgiveness and be given a second chance, ***every time they sin against us.***

In a nutshell, the compassionate love makes you to love your spouse even when he or she becomes unlovable by the "not so good" things he or she does to you, and that is what the merciful God did to you and me; and the whole world for that matter through His only begotten son, Christ Jesus.

Another interesting story is that, patriarch Abraham lied and gave away his wife two times. I could only imagine that traumatizing situation for Sarah, and she is the one who felt it and could tell it all better than myself; but God intervened in both occasions. ***God can intervene in any marriage relationship situation, just have faith and believe in Him.*** Continue to believe His promises to you about you and you'll be just fine. What does the Scripture say? "Abraham believed God, and it was accounted to him for righteousness." (Rom. 4:3). Another secret about faith is that of calling things which are not as though they were. (Rom. 4:17).

All God's promises to you and the things that you hope for, faith becomes the substance that you hold and the evidence that you see until those things materialize. God's promises to you are yes and amen. This is what patriarch Abraham believed, and every believer in God should do likewise in order to be counted as righteous. When you are righteous, God will order your footsteps. The Holy Writ also says that, the effectual fervent prayer of the righteous availeth much; in other words, it overcomes. (James 5:16). The two verses listed below are examples of other God's promises.

"... I will never leave you nor forsake you."
(Heb. 13:5).

"Jesus Christ is the same yesterday, today, and forever."
(Heb. 13:8).

It is a fact that information makes you think, and its effect is mind-blowing; but revelation makes you worship in humble adoration to God, and its effect makes you to come closer to Him. Once you have a revelation of who God is to you, that will influence you to love Him in return. It is also crucial to have a revelation or understanding of who your partner is to you in the marriage relationship.

Now, let's go back to our marriage relationships and reflect. ***There are moments when one becomes emotionally torn apart when it comes to some of the five senses, and that should be the time that the "Super Sense" takes over to find the solutions that the natural senses could not obtain.*** Other people have given up in this regard because they did not have the "Super Sense", or even believe in it as a workable solution to life's challenges.

Through the "Super Sense" you can Taste God, Touch God, Smell God, See God and also Hear from God. The natural senses are a bit carnal in nature, and that is why they will fail to tap into the supernatural in order to get you the solutions or divine intervention that you need for your challenges. It is only by faith that you can Taste Heaven, Touch Heaven, Smell Heaven, See Heaven and even Hear from Heaven; but carnally this may sound nonsensical.

"Jesus said unto him, If thou canst believe, all things are possible to him that believeth."
(Mk 9:23).

Now you can see what God's specialty is, He specializes on those things thought impossible by human reasoning; even our marriage relationships are not spared. God can zoom in there to turn things around and make the impossible things possible if we allow Him through faith. ***The God that I serve can make rivers flow in the desert,*** remember Ezekiel and the valley of dry bones. (Ezekiel 37:1-14).

"And Jesus looking upon them said, with men it is impossible, but not with God; for with God all things are possible." (Mk 10:27).

God has no limitations concerning what He can do for us in our marriage relationships, even the so called irretrievable marriage-breakdown is nothing for Him not to solve. ***God's intervention can change any situation upside down.*** Jehovah Jireh knows no limits when He has to provide and He has no equal, He is the unlimited God. All we need to do is to invite Him so that He becomes present in our lives. He says, *"Behold, I stand at the door and knock. If anyone hears My voice and opens the door, I will come in to him and dine with him, and he with Me."* (Rev 3:20 NKJV).

"Because of the privilege and authority God has given me, I give each of you this warning: Don't think you are better than you really are. Be honest in your evaluation of yourselves, measuring yourselves by the faith God has given us." (Rom 12:3). So, faith is given to us by God Himself. Above all, let faith be the measuring stick of the goodness, health and strength of our lifestyles.

18 *"Come now, let us reason together," says the LORD. "Though your sins are like scarlet, they will be as white as snow; though they are as red as crimson, they will become like wool.* 19 If you are willing and obedient, you will eat the best of the land. 20 *But if you resist and rebel, you will be devoured by the sword." For the mouth of the LORD has spoken."*
(Isa 1:18-20 BSB).

"The days are coming," says the Lord God, "when I will send a time upon the land when the people will be very hungry. They will not be hungry for bread or thirsty for water, but they will be hungry to hear the Words of the Lord." (Amos 8:11 NLV).

There are many limitations on carnality, carnality cannot quench the spiritual thirst, neither can it fill the spiritual hunger. That's the reason why a carnal person is living an imbalanced life.

"But the person who is not a Christian does not understand these words from the Holy Spirit. He thinks they are foolish. He cannot understand them because he does not have the Holy Spirit to help him understand." (1 Cor. 2:14 NLV). A carnal man cannot even understand God's things. God's paramount challenge to mankind is "Knowing Him".

God knows you and your marriage relationship better than yourself and before you even claim to know Him. He says, *"I know the plans I have for you."* (Jeremiah 29:11). He knows the plans He has for you with your marriage relationship included.

Remember that some of the best blessings come out of the worst situations in marriage relationships. So, don't give up easily in any difficult situation, God already has the solution but it is not visible to you just yet; however, you should do what you have to do believing that God will provide you with the solution. Just like Patriarch Abraham who told his son Isaac that God would provide the lamb of sacrifice, and God did. Christianity is a relationship and not just a religion for us to subscribe to. ***Everyone can be religious and yet not have a relationship with the Living God.***

There will be those moments in life when you have to struggle with doubt, and what will matter most at that moment is the rock-solid relationship you have with the Most-High God through faith. The paramount challenge to you today is, do you accept God's challenge to believe in Him by faith today? He wants to be part of your life, He wants to be part of your marriage relationship. Jesus had to get into the private affairs of the Samaritan woman in order to help her. So, for your own marriage to be helped, He has to get into your private affairs. He already knows everything, but it's a matter of you allowing Him to get in and help, because He does not force Himself into couple's affairs. He stands at the door and knock.

Let me say this, if the situation is so serious and desperate such that you need something you never had in your marriage relationship right now, you may have to do something positive you've never done before, in order to get the desired result. You might be attending church services, or one might be singing in the worship team or playing some kind of role in church; but, do you have a "rock-solid" relationship with God? That is His paramount challenge to you. Again, you might have to do something you've never done in order to get what you strongly wish for. Just like the prodigal son, you need to take a step in the right direction, and the Heavenly Father is always waiting in love to receive you on the home side. Remember, ***faith in God, often times defies the logic and achieve the impossible result.***

Jesus said, *"Come to me all ye that are weary and heavy laden, I will give you rest."* In your mind and heart allow the power behind these words to bring freedom, peace and tranquility in your life and also set all your captives free. Allow the creative power loaded in the Word of God to create a new spirit and a new life in your marriage relationship. The same creative power that was behind the words, *"Let there be light"* in the book of Genesis, is the same creative power loaded in the words of Jesus Christ as stated above.

In Genesis, God's words were so loaded and power packed such that at the mention of those words, darkness had to leave at the light's calling to appear. So, don't bother much about rebuking and chasing demons of darkness away, just call the light Christ Jesus to appear in your life and marriage; and then darkness will have to leave and give way to the light. In reality, the two cannot coexist. Yes, they can't be in the same place at the same time, one has to leave.

I trust you understand His paramount challenge to you today, and the need for you to match His commitment to your life with equal reciprocity. This is His paramount challenge to you and your partner, so that you live the current and future marriage life as fortified as you should. Are you up to the challenge? I hope you are.

ANALOGY QUIZ: THE PARAMOUNT CHALLENGE			
No.	**ASSESSMENT STATEMENTS** (where 10 is most likely and 5 means it needs some tender loving attention)	**10**	**5**
1.	I understand what is God's paramount challenge to me.		
2.	My partner understands what is God's paramount challenge to him or her.		
3.	I have accepted God's paramount challenge to me.		
4.	My partner has accepted God's paramount challenge to him or her.		
5.	I have allowed God to be present and be part of our relationship.		
6.	My partner has allowed God to be part and be present in our relationship.		
7.	I believe that God has a plan for our marriage relationship.		
8.	God has given me a measure of faith to believe in Him for the things beyond my control.		
9.	God has given my partner a measure of faith to believe in Him for the things beyond my partner's control.		
10.	I have secured the "Super Sense" to be part of my life.		
11.	My partner has secured the "Super Sense" to be part his or her life.		

12.	By God's help the "Super Sense" will make me go beyond my limitations every time I deal with my marital challenges.		
13.	I'm prepared to do positive things I've never done before in order to get the desired results for our marriage relationship.		
14.	My partner is prepared to do positive things he/she's never done before in order to get the desired results for our marriage relationship.		
15.	I take God's paramount challenge to me and my partner seriously.		
16.	I believe in God's creative and power packed Word to change my life and my marriage relationship for the better.		
17.	My partner believes in God's creative and power packed Word to change his or her life and our marriage relationship for the better.		
18.	Calling the light Christ Jesus to appear into my life and marriage relationship will cause darkness to pack and go, and there's no possibility of their coexistence. (light and darkness).		
19.	God's paramount challenge to mankind is loud and clear to me.		
20.	Yes, I can now confidently say that the weapons of our marriage warfare are not carnal but they are mighty through God.		

Quiz Notes:
The quiz has 20 items, having an overall score of 200 means you are doing just fine in the *"element"* as far as the 20 items are concerned; and there is minimal enhancement or improvement that needs to be done. A score of 180 (90%) means tender loving attention is required on all items with a score of 5. A score of 160 (80%) and below means that quite a bit of work has to be done, because 20% or more of the items have scored 5 points each instead of 10. One may not comfortably say they have mastered or internalized God's Paramount Challenge in their relationship.

One has to do some serious introspection, and then further engage in a meaningful dialogue with the spouse about this. If things seem to be overwhelming, you still have the professional counselor or your local pastor on your side for guidance. Remember, the quiz is not the counselor or pastor, it only gives clues as to say, among others, what things you need to consider in your endeavor of internalizing God's Paramount Challenge in the lives of the partners in the relationship.

CHAPTER 21

WHAT THE FUTURE HOLDS?

When you finally think you've mastered the elements of good and happy marriages for your own relationship, just think of the rich young ruler who mastered all the ten commandments from childhood, but failed the test that Jesus gave to him; because he was not ready and willing to do what he had to do next. ***The future of every couple is unpredictable and the marriage context or the environment within which the couples live their marriage is rapidly changing with the times.*** That becomes a call for married couples to be better prepared to face the unknown and unpredictable tough challenges of the future.

This also calls for vigilance and flexibility amongst couples, to continuously learn new ways to work on their relationships in order to keep them healthy, strong and happy. This kind of attitude will make the couples to realize future successes as well. Some of the relevant issues have been addressed in my second book, *"Navigating the Stormy Seas of Marriage Life"* which will be published soon.

The reality is that we may not know what the future holds, but we may get to know who holds the future. We may not be certain about the future of our marriages, but we may be certain about who holds their future. You may not be aware what tomorrow may bring, but you can be sure and be attached to the one who determines tomorrow.

We may not possess the insight, intelligence and percipience to see the future of our marriage relationships, but God can give us power and wisdom to plan and work on the sustenance of our marriages.

It takes action for something to be accomplished. Bear in mind, in Him, we can do ALL things because with Him ALL things are possible. What I mean is that, with God's guidance and support, your future should be sorted. (Mark 10:27).

I have discovered that the marriage context is so vast and dynamic, and one can never be exhaustive in its discussion. This book is just a drop in the ocean for that kind of engagement or commitment. This also paves a way for future books that I will have to write to encourage the sustenance of marriage relationships. The main aim of this book has been to encourage and energize a healthy dialogue amongst the married couples, with regards to the contextual matters affecting their marriage relationships. While such matters have been articulated and alluded to in the book, the couples may revisit them as often as they wish for their indulgence and fulfilment, in pursuit of happiness and goodness in their relationships.

I am of the view that through this book, those couples who are already in happy marriages, will get the portion that will further motivate them to carry on even further happily. Those in struggling relationships will find the added strength and confidence that they need to never give up on their marriages. Those in serious and sensitive situations, will be revived to give their marriage relationships another chance to survive. ***Honestly speaking, our marriage relationships go through a lot, that's why they'll always deserve a chance after another.***

I also hope that this book will put more fuel to the zeal of the seasoned and upcoming writers to do more work on the subject of marriage relationships. Another reality is that the elements of good and happy marriages affect the emotional, mental and physical well-being of those involved in marriage relationships. Hence it is crucial to have a good understanding of them as married couples.

Every spouse has been encouraged to learn to be non-defensive in response to each other, with the aim of changing the unwanted behavior where possible. ***One learns to change or unlearn the wrong behavior, on one's own accord rather than being forced, hence I believe change to be a process.***

The focus should be to commit to improve in the areas of weakness and make some enhancements in those areas that are strong. The idea is that this should be possibly done together by the partners, so that they can support each other in the process. It can be a bit disappointing not to get support from your partner when trying to do an enhancement to an element of a good and happy marriage; only to find out that the other partner was not aware of what you were trying to do. Diversified synergy between the partners is encouraged and is key, even when looking into the future, the elements of good and happy marriage will always be part of the marriage context. In other words, they will always be part of the life time survival of the marriage relationships even for ages to come.

The rock-solid relationship with the Most-High God is highly recommended as the crucial part of one's personal life, because as human beings, we have limitations such that divine intervention is necessary to balance our lives; without that kind of intervention our marriage relationships remain imbalanced and highly vulnerable to all kinds of attacks, especially the spiritual attacks.

Having read about the elements in discussion, the decision making still remains with the married couples about what to do with their marriage relationships when challenges assail. My aim is to help by encouraging you to be a better unique you in your own relationship. So, your aim should be to help your partner to be a better unique partner in the relationship. What is there in the future are challenges and successes that couples have to go through, ***the winning secret is in getting yourselves prepared.*** Never get weary in investing in your marriage relationship by reading motivating and inspiring books, from authors who are passionate on the survival and sustenance of marriage relationships. Bear in mind, that is just one thing among many that you still need to do for your marriage relationship.

May the Almighty grant you and your partner the wisdom you need to make and keep your marriage to be one of the good, successful and happy marriages existing in the world, and for others around you to learn from. This is another way for you to leave a good heritage and legacy. Shalom!

www.ingramcontent.com/pod-product-compliance
Lightning Source LLC
Chambersburg PA
CBHW051417090426
42737CB00014B/2708